MEXICO'S
SCHOOL-MADE
SOCIETY

MEXICO'S SCHOOL - MADE SOCIETY

BY

GEORGE C. BOOTH

GREENWOOD PRESS, PUBLISHERS
NEW YORK

DEDICATED TO

E. B. BOOTH

WHOSE UNDERSTANDING AND HELP

MADE THIS WORK POSSIBLE

PREFACE

CITIZENS of the United States are becoming more and more conscious of their neighbor south of the Rio Bravo. They are watching the social and economic moves that are being made in Mexico, and they are keenly interested in understanding the underlying theories that motivate these changes. Mexico is explained and denounced and praised in an augmenting stream of books, pamphlets, and magazine articles. Journals of all the leading educational societies of the country have carried accounts of what is being done in Mexico and of how it is being carried out. But daily newspapers contain dispatches that leave the reader confused as to the aims of the sister republic. And little has been written about why Mexico has shown such a sudden interest in education and what she expects to accomplish by it.

THE PROBLEM

The purpose of this study, then, is to outline the philosophy of the developing "Socialist schools" of Mexico, and the means by which this philosophy is to be translated into action. More than that, it attempts to show how and why this philosophy developed.

The term "Socialist," as applied to the schools of Mexico and to the system as a whole, is part of the official nomenclature; it is not a descriptive adjective arbitrarily applied by the author. Once the underlying bases of Mexican Scientific Socialism have been made clear, historically and ideologically, the more specific philosophy of the school system will be shown and the various techniques of the schools will be presented to show what the Mexicans are doing to attain the goals they have set for themselves.

Data for the critique of Mexican methods of study were gathered from four main sources: historical works; materials dealing with the official philosophy of Mexico contained in publications issued by those close to the Secretary of Education; conferences with Department Chiefs in the Secretariat; and visits to schools in various parts of the republic.

Historical research was carried on largely in the United States, although the Biblioteca Nacional of Mexico City was also drawn upon. Items included a few manuscripts and, more particularly, certain little-known books, both Spanish and Mexican, which are almost unobtainable elsewhere. Several books consulted in the Biblioteca Nacional have had, and are having, a strong influence upon the thinkers of Mexico. These books are translations from the Russian and are coming to Mexico continually. The directors of the Henry E. Huntington Library kindly allowed the author the use of their valuable collection of early Mexican manuscripts.

In order to get an exact interpretation of the official philosophy of the Federal Schools the author spent two summers in Mexico City collecting printed matter. This material consisted of some dozen books published within the past three years, innumerable brochures, *programas,* outlines, pamphlets, and periodicals. He subscribed to certain magazines and has had *El Maestro Rural, Simiente,* and *La Revista de Educación* since their inception. Conferences in Mexico City with chiefs and subchiefs of all the departments concerned in this study took place. The men at the head of Mexico's educational destinies have proved themselves to be courteous, polished, and well-trained. Especially valuable was a series of discussions with Dr. Manuel R. Palacios, Chief of the Department of Socialist Orientation. Dr. Palacios was also President of the Third Inter-American Conference of Education held in Mexico City from August 22 to 29, 1937. This conference proved to be highly valuable in demonstrating the methods by which the Mexicans establish their programs through the co-operative thinking of their leaders. Here also the author had the privilege of meeting many regional and state directors of education.

Visits to other parts of Mexico helped to shape the concept of the many components of Mexican education into a whole. In Hermosillo, Sonora, the author was invited to attend sessions of an institute staged by the Federación de Maestros Socialistas. Their successful *huelga*—strike—of twenty-four hours also presented a view of that little-used weapon. Sitting with the members of the Cultural Missions at their training classes gave the author an insight into the problems of these remarkable modern missionaries, who carry the torch of learning to the lowest cultural levels in the country—the Tarahumare, the Seri, the Yaqui, the Cora, and other Indians in the most inaccessible parts.

As time limitations forbade visits to all the states of the republic, the author attempted to study the schools in action in parts that would be typical of all Mexico. Part of the national plan is to adapt education to the locale. Students are taught to adapt themselves to their particular environment. While Mexico is a land of many climates and many distinct local cultures, it may be divided into broad geographical sectors that have common problems.

The traditional division is to separate the country into *tierra caliente,* the hot country; *tierra templada,* the temperate country; and *tierra fría,* the cold country. If the economic factor is considered, it is more convenient to study the land as divided into other categories: The northern states, Sonora, Chihuahua, Coahuila, and parts of Tamaulipas and Nuevo Leon are extensive plains which are partially desert. Here cattle raising and mining are the chief industries, with little handicraft in evidence. The central plateau region is the part that is considered as *México típico,* with colorful handicrafts, agriculture, and mining predominant. The low-lying coastal plains and southern Mexico are afflicted with intense heat and malarial swamps, but at the same time are rich in timber, coffee, vanilla, and other tropical products. In his travels the author has attempted to study each locale as thoroughly as possible to see whether or not the schools are actually carrying out the programs of the Secretariat and whether or not the program is actually applicable to the situation if followed.

CONTENTS

xi

Chapter I

THE PHILOSOPHY OF SOCIALIST EDUCATION

THE BASIS of the Mexican Socialist school of today is the famous Article 3 as revised by the convention of the Partido Nacional Revolucionario (National Revolutionary Party, often cited as P.N.R.) at Querétaro in October 1933. Article 3 of the Constitution of 1917 reads:

Instruction is free; that given in public institutions of learning shall be secular. Primary instruction, whether higher or lower, given in private institutions, shall likewise be secular. Private primary schools may be established only subject to official supervision. Primary instruction in public institutions shall be gratuitous.[1]

Under the provisions of this article, education in Mexico has continued to improve but has taken on the character of each successive Secretary of Public Education, so that educational styles have marked the schools strongly. One central theme which may be noted in the schools after 1917 is the socialization of the group rather than the development of individualism. The effect of John Dewey was felt for a number of years in the "schools of action."

[1] *The Mexican Constitution of 1917 Compared with the Constitution of 1857,* translated and arranged by H. N. Branch (Supplement to *The Annals of the American Academy of Political and Social Science,* May 1917).

There was also the period of the *casa del pueblo,* the house of the people, when adult education received a strong impetus. The "open-air school," with its strong swing toward physical education, followed the introduction of *vitalismo,* behaviorism. In all of this experimental education the actual educators formulated their theories and planned their organization.

SOCIALISM CONSTITUTIONAL IN MEXICO

The convening of the Partido Nacional Revolucionario at Querétaro brought into expression a concept new to Mexico—the frank belief that education is the monopoly of all the people of the state, not of a group, whether that group be of the Church or of the body of professional educators. Its leaders went back to a materialist interpretation of history and pointed out that education has always been oriented by the dominant classes, that it has attempted to mold the human being into the ideal of the period, and that the basis of education in all ages has been economic. Therefore the members of the convention determined, from the standpoint of laymen and legislators, what the aims and limits of education should be. They amended Article 3 to read:

ARTICLE 3. The education imparted by the State shall be a socialistic one and, in addition to excluding all religious doctrine, shall combat fanaticism and prejudices by organizing its instruction and activities in a way that shall permit the creation in youth of an exact and rational concept of the Universe and of social life.

Only the State—Federation, States, Municipalities—shall impart primary, secondary, and normal education. Authorization may be conceded to individuals who desire to impart education in any of the aforementioned three levels in conformity, in every case, with the following norms:

I. The teachings and activities of private plants must adjust themselves without exception to that indicated in the initial paragraph of this Article and shall be in charge of persons who, in the opinion of the State, shall have sufficient professional preparation and a morality and ideology that is suitable to and in keeping with this precept. In view of this, religious corporations, the ministers of cults, the organizations which preferably or exclusively carry on educational activities, and the associations or societies bound directly or indirectly to the propaganda of a religious creed shall in no way intervene in primary, secondary, or normal schools, nor shall they be permitted to assist these financially.

II. The formation of plans, programmes, and methods of teaching shall in every case rest in the State.

III. Private plants shall not be permitted to function without first, and in each case, having obtained the express authorization of the public power.

IV. The State may at any time revoke the authorization granted (to private individuals or organizations). There shall be no judgment or recourse whatsoever against such revocation.

The same norms shall govern the education of whatever type or grade that is imparted to workers or peasants.

Primary education shall be obligatory, and the State shall impart it gratuitously.

The State may, at its discretion and at any time, withdraw recognition of official validity to the studies made in private plants.

The Congress of the Union, in the interest of unifying and co-ordinating education throughout the Republic, shall promulgate the necessary laws destined to distribute the social educative function between the Federation and the States and Municipalities, to fix the financial apportionments corresponding to that public service, and to indicate the sanctions (penalties) applicable to those functionaries who do not comply with, or force compliance to, the respective dispositions, as well as to all those who violate them.[2]

So new was this line of thought, and so definitely aimed at the Catholic Church, that it raised an immediate storm

[2] George I. Sanchez, translator, *Mexico: A Revolution by Education* (The Viking Press, 1939), pp. 102–3.

of protest from the clergy. The Chamber of Deputies debated the change for a week, even considering a motion to substitute the word "Marxist" for "Socialist"; but on October 10, 1933, it voted unanimously to alter the Constitution and apply Article 3 to all schools from the kindergarten to the university, leaving the latter autonomous.

The Catholic Church threw all of its influence against the enforcement of the reforms. On January 17, 1934, a circular letter was sent out to be read in all Catholic churches on January 20, calling for a school strike on the ground that only parents, Catholic teachers, and priests were acceptable as teachers of Catholic children. Four fundamental principles were embodied in the letter: no Catholic can be a Socialist; no Catholic can study or teach Socialism; no Catholic can condone Socialism; and no Catholic can approve pedagogic naturalism or sex education.[3]

MEANING OF MEXICAN, OR SCIENTIFIC, SOCIALISM

The provisions of Article 3, in the thinking of the National Revolutionary Party, took education out of the field of speculative philosophy and placed it in the field of applied sciences. The *plan sexenal,* or six-year plan, which was drafted at the same time, provided for realistic reforms in the field of land distribution, better exploitation of natural resources, and expropriation of heavy industries and the remaining *haciendas.* The educational provisions were so closely integrated with this program that it is difficult, if not impossible, to draw a line between its provisions for education and those for economic reform. "The chief interest of the Mexican government in the unification of the schools is in the firm establishment of its

[3] "Socialism and Catholicism in the Mexican Schools," *School and Society,* 43: 111, January 25, 1936.

modern ideology," says Dr. Manuel R. Palacios.[4] To the cry for academic freedom the ideologists reply that at no time have schools or individuals had freedom of teaching or thought. For proof they again go back to Marx and economic determinism. According to this theory, each period or economic stage had its own ideal of what the adult should be and every device of society was used to mold the child to this ideal. In the Middle Ages the chief emphasis of society was on "otherworldliness" and all agencies of society were subordinated to the Church and its work of preparing for a life to come. This line of reasoning postulated that teachers did not have academic freedom, for their thinking was conditioned by the state, which in this case was the Church. In the period of the Renaissance a different ideal took form—that of the individual who could enrich himself unrestrainedly at the expense of society. This enrichment could be economic, religious, or cultural. In this period the individual flourished in all fields—Leonardo da Vinci in art, Niccolo Machiavelli in politics, Francis Drake in the field of glorified piracy. Since then, in the era of capitalism, money, per se, has been raised to the point of prime importance. As a result, education in capitalist countries places its emphasis on training for money-making or some other form of financial or material success for the individual. In each case, the modern Mexican ideologist reasons, there has been no "freedom of teaching." The teacher has been free only to teach in his own way what society has demanded.

These very same individual techniques tend to add to the student's training in individualism, which the Socialist considers merely a form of selfishness. Socialization is not

[4] M. R. Palacios, "Principles Underlying Mexican Education," *Progressive Education,* 12:83, February 1936.

an isolated compartment of knowledge that can be taught by individualists; it is a method of living that must be absorbed by the individual, whether he be adult or student. The teachers must first of all be socialized themselves before they can add to the socialization of the child, to accomplish which purpose they must form an educational program in accord with the social program as formulated by the representatives of all groups in society. These programs, then, are co-operative plans worked out as the result of scientific data collected and assimilated. They are the matured thinking of large groups of trained men and women. Once they have been accepted, it seems to the Socialist that it is the duty of the individual to study the program and fit himself and his thinking into the social order. Where, then, he asks, is there room for liberty of teaching if it implies that the individual is so conceited as to think his own methods superior to those of society?[5]

The state and the school.—The Socialist state is not considered paramount to the individual, as is the Fascist state. The state is considered in the same light as is the brain in the individual. It decides what course the body is to follow and then sends messages through the effectors to the various members of the body. The Socialist state is looked upon as an evolutionary growth out of and beyond the despotic and liberal state. In the despotic state the members are ordered about for the final good, and at the whim, of one man or, at best, a small group of selfish individuals. In the liberal state the citizens are given as much freedom of choice as possible. Each of these states is equally planless and aimless, say the Socialists. In the first the blind drive of selfishness will brutalize the individual

---

[5] Trejo Lerdo de Tejada, *La Educación Socialista*, p. 214; also *Plan Sexenal del Partido Nacional Revolucionario,* translated as *The Mexican Government's Six-Year Plan,* p. 18.

more and more until the national median is so low that the nation will be destroyed through sheer cumulative ignorance. In the liberal state the individuals who are intelligent or trained will succeed, but the untrained classes will sink lower as the whole population did in the despotic state. Finally the time will come when they will lower the culture sufficiently to cause the breakdown of the country. An activating state is, then, a necessity for carrying out the Socialist program. This *Estado actuante* means more than a state that moves to action; it means a state that directs the movement according to a definite thesis.

. . . . in the Mexican revolutionary concept, the state is an active agent of management and direction of the vital phenomena of the country; not a mere custodian of national integrity, peace, and public order.[6]

Here is the definite split between the Socialist and the Fascist philosophies. The Socialist thesis is established by the co-operative work of sociologists and scientists, who gather data and apply the laws of science to their findings.[7] A plan is worked out for the betterment of society, and for the betterment of the state. The state then has the duty of carrying out the program in a strong, uncompromising manner. An important point is the belief that the goals for society and for the state must be the same.

Social inertia, which is compounded of individual ignorance, traditionalism, and special interests, will attempt to hold back the program. For this reason the Socialist state depends strongly on education: The school is not a thing apart; it is as much at the call of the government as is the army:

The primary school is a social institution and, as such, its teachings and the conditions to be fulfilled by teachers, in order

[6] *The Mexican Government's Six-Year Plan*, p. 17.
[7] L. S. Ponton, *Hacia la Escuela Socialista*, p. 39.

to comply with the social function must be those set by the state as the genuine and direct representative of the people at large; no right being conceded to private individuals (who have a false and exaggerated idea of individual liberty) to organize and manage schools independently of State control.[8]

Education is looked to as the instrument of enlightenment which will prepare the people to understand the program and then carry it out. The Socialist theory does not depend on force to make its program work; it depends on the mass of the people. It is believed that once the people understand what is being done for them they will allow no interference.[9]

Certain phrases which fit into this philosophy are heard continually. Such phrases are "class solidarity," "united front," and the "struggle of classes." The *lucha de clases,* or struggle of classes, is a struggle largely of ideas. As the Socialists do not depend on force, they consider its use as a sign of the breakdown of logic. To be consistent they must allow freedom of speech and of the press to both the traditionalist and the Socialist. The reason for such a policy is obvious. According to their own theory, false doctrines are supported by force and true doctrines triumph by their own virtue. The Socialist program is divided into two parts. The first part consists in fomenting the class struggle and in raising the cultural level of the people; eventually, it is believed, there will be but one class, and then each individual can be helped to work toward his highest capabilities. The second part of the program has to do with society when the first stage is reached.

The equalization of man.—Perhaps the one front on which the Scientific Socialists have endured the most as-

[8] *The Mexican Government's Six-Year Plan,* pp. 30–31.
[9] M. R. Palacios, *op. cit.,* p. 81.

saults is that of their insistence that society must work toward equalization, *igualación*. Mexican scientific philosophers maintain that these attacks are occasioned by enemies who do not understand their thesis or who do not want to understand it. Briefly, they do not believe that men are equal in intellectual or psychological characteristics today. They do not know that they can ever be. But they do believe that they are equal in demanding certain rights from society. They believe that by the application of sound sociological and educational principles to society there will be more of an equalization of privileges. With the equalization of privileges, including proper living and study, the individual will become a well-rounded and happy person developed more nearly to his full capabilities. This belief is an attempt to validate scientifically the philosophic concept known as "perfectionism," postulated by Condorcet and carried to lyric heights by the poet Shelley.

The German political writer, Max Scheler, is author of the statement that equalization is the keynote of the modern epoch. His influence is acknowledged by the Mexicans, who agree with his handling of the problem. Scheler says that there are three phases of modern equalization: ethnologic, psychologic, and economic.

1. *Ethnic equalization.*—Among sociologists and psychologists the theory of racial differences is being widely modified. The idea of "lesser breeds without the law" is coming to be considered a Nordic rationalization. For instance, the speed with which Japan had accepted and adapted Western techniques has proved that national conditioning does exist. China, Turkey, and India, as rapidly as they can acquire the specific training necessary, become as proficient as the Occident in techniques of industry, warfare, and science. The United States is cited as an example of a country which has amalgamated many races

and cultures into a distinct type. For centuries Spain maintained the belief that the indigenous races of Mexico were so inferior that they were fit only to be beasts of burden. Yet thousands of examples are extant of an Indian's mastering a material or intellectual technique and equaling the Spaniard. In the fields of art, handicrafts, theology, and metallurgy this tendency has been especially noted; and it gives the Mexican of today cause to believe that the many ethnic groups of Mexico can be raised to a level of national culture equal to that of any in the world.[10]

2. *Psychologic equalization.*—The belief in equalization has been given a tremendous impetus by the spread of behavioristic psychology. Pavlov is known as well in Mexico as in Russia. The effect of behaviorism, *vitalismo,* is the keynote of a great part of the educational philosophy. This theory makes the nervous system the essential cause of behavior—any biologic unit may be conditioned to react in a desired way by applying the concomitant stimulus. A study of biology convinces the behaviorist that since all human beings have the same nervous system they may eventually be trained to react in the same way. In the past, "mind" was considered as a thing apart from the body, and an attempt was made to train it as an isolated entity. The belief was almost universal that certain persons had better minds than others because of a mystic form of "original endowment." For the same reason, certain nations were endowed more fortunately than other nations.[11] "Original nature" was discussed at great length and conditioned the type of religious belief and education that a nation might have. Certain instincts were believed to re-

---

[10] L. S. Ponton, *op. cit.,* pp. 24 ff.; also Manuel Gamio, "Incorporating the Indian in the Mexican Population," in *Aspects of Mexican Civilization,* by José Vasconcelos and Manuel Gamio.

[11] Nicolas Bujarin, *El Materialismo Histórico,* p. 263.

side in the babe at birth, and nothing could change these instincts. Certain religions taught that man was born in sin and must spend his entire life in an unhappy, unnatural manner in an attempt to expiate this sin.

Behaviorism has opened a new field of optimism to its followers, for it denies the existence of an original nature outside of the limits of the nervous system. It denies the existence of instincts and does not recognize great racial differences. For these reasons the Mexican Socialist places great faith in changes he has made in the national educational structure.[12] Some of these changes based on behaviorism affect his methods as to physical education, dietetics, science or naturalistic education, and vocational training. These activities are expected to give full expression to the body and the nervous system, allowing for expression rather than repression. The aim of *vitalismo* is the *ser plenario,* the "full man," the full and complete life for the individual.[13]

The creed opposed to that of socialization of all the people is individualism. Individualism points to its men of genius during the ages as a proof that all men can never be equal and that they should not be because of the enormous contributions of genius. The behaviorist answers that the genius is merely an index of what more men could be if inhibiting social factors were removed. Furthermore, he says, it is a goal which all men may reach if society is sufficiently perfected.

Oddly enough, the Scientific Socialist of Mexico does not deny the existence of the spiritual side of man's nature. He does deny the alleged dichotomous nature of man, according to which body and spirit are two separate factors. As the sociologist aims to unify society so that

[12] *Consejo de Educación Primaria del D. F.,* pp. 19 ff.
[13] L. S. Ponton, *op. cit.,* p. 51.

there will be no conflicting social forces, the psychologist aims at psychological unity. The *ser plenario* will have the physical and spiritual parts of his being fused into an integrated whole.

El fin de la educación es aquí, nuevamente, LA FORMACIÓN DE LA PERSONALIDAD, PERO MEDÍANTE LA INTERACCIÓN DE LOS DOS ELEMENTOS QUE ANTES APARECÍAN SEPARADOS E INDEPENDIENTES.[14]

3. *Economic equalization.*—The tendency toward economic equalization is marked by the continued class struggle, declare the Marxian philosophers. They see the existence of classes as the outgrowth of castes and classes in primitive society, where the privileged acquired their prestige in two ways. Either they took the best of everything by virtue of brute strength, as did the tribal chieftains; or they acquired it by exploiting the ignorance and fear of their fellows, as did medicine men and magicians. The two types of exploiters have worked hand in glove ever since, say the Marxians. Ancient monarchies kept the class lines distinct by the use of ignorance and fear— ignorance of the true facts of life and society, and fear of the king's might. The priesthood upheld the fiction by insisting that the king had certain divine rights which it was sacrilege to resist. To keep itself in a privileged position the priesthood has found it necessary to make the people believe in an utterly false cosmogony. Every device of priest and king has always been brought to bear on ideas tending to disprove the divine right of king and priest to exploit, say the Marxians.

Dynasties have been overthrown and successful revolutions have been staged; but the class system remains. How do the Marxian theorists explain this anomaly? They

---

[14] L. S. Ponton, *op. cit.,* p. 52 (capitals as in original).

simply point out that the elementary force that has never been destroyed is the economic motive for exploitation. Theoretically, the French Revolution should have established equality, for equality was the second of the three famous words of the slogan: Liberty, equality, and fraternity. However, nothing but names were destroyed. The French peasant and worker merely acquired a new set of masters. As long as the economic motive for individual profit remains, the class struggle must go on; so the way out is to socialize all the means of production and to perfect methods of distribution in order to resolve the struggle. In the meantime, the school in Mexico is the medium which directs the struggle, pointing out to the students their rights and duties and the methods available for attacking intrenched privilege.[15] The Church is attacked as a deleterious economic factor, not as a spiritual force. The state and the school encourage spiritual and religious development, but not of a fanatic, supernatural, or antirationalistic nature.[16]

PREMISES OF SOCIALIST EDUCATIONAL THEORY

It has been pointed out in what way the Constitution was amended to include Socialist education, in what way Socialist education is interpreted, and the inevitability of the coming of the Socialist state because of the class struggle. The question which next arises is, what is the ideal type set up by Socialism and how is the average child to be molded into the similitude of the prototype? To answer that question it becomes necessary to study the rights and duties of the child under the Socialist state and the duties and functions of the teacher or *maestro,* and then what the action of the Socialist school and the *ma-*

[15] Emilio Portes Gil, *La Escuela y el Campesino,* pp. 29 f.
[16] George I. Sanchez, *op. cit.,* chapter viii.

estro upon the child born in the Socialist society should be. It must be kept in mind constantly that the Mexican school is considered primarily social—that it is an instrument of the state to condition the environment of the child scientifically so that he will develop into a man distinct from the man of the past:

La Escuela Socialista debe ser un factor determinante del nuevo orden social y económico de Mexico y para ello debe participar de un modo intenso y extenso en la vida misma de la comunidad ...[17]

Rights and duties of the child.—The Mexican ideology resolves the philosophical debate as to who owns the child, the family or society, by answering that neither owns him. He is a free member of society from the moment he is born, and he is under a reciprocal agreement with both the family and society. He has certain inalienable rights which must be respected by the family, by society, and by the state. On the other hand, he has duties which he must discharge faithfully if he is to merit and receive his right:

He has a right to all the benefits that Humanity has acquired through the ages.

The child has the right to issue from healthy parents who are capable of transmitting maximum vitality to him, and to be born under hygienic conditions free from conditions that will hinder his development.

The parents must bring to matrimony the fullest knowledge of the problems of conjugal life and of the growth and education of children.

The child must be placed in an environment where he will develop physically and intellectually in a normal manner.

The hungry child must be fed, the sick, nourished; the retarded must be stimulated, the wayward, guided; the orphan and the abandoned must be protected. The child must be the first to receive aid in times of calamity.

All children must be given the chance to reach the cultural

[17] J. J. de la Rosa P., *La Escuela Socialista Mexicana*, p. 60.

level they are capable of, independently of circumstances of an economic, ethnic, religious, or social nature.

The child has the right to be the agent of his own education, and to feel the pleasure of investigation and the discovery of truth. He will be aided and guided in thus forming his own culture.

It is the right of the child that his mentality be respected and that he shall not have imposed upon him fanatical or prejudiced ideas or concepts of life that hinder or impede his formation of a sane consciousness. His interests, necessities, and spontaneous activities must be respected, for it is from these that he acquires the feeling of responsibility towards collective society, and reaches the maximum evolution of his personality and aptitudes. The child has possibilities that must be discovered, evolved and cultivated. It is necessary that he reach complete self-direction in searching for and directing himself toward the cause of things.

He has a right to have revolutionary teachers of high character and vocational training who do not consider their position simply as a means toward a livelihood but who think in terms of Socialistic ideals of advance.

He has a right to a simple, local school that is a happy, hygienic place which he helps to improve and keep in order.

All children have a right to the open air for their work, to play their games, take natural exercises and respiratory movements which constitute their best forms of physical education; to receive an education of the body that habituates them to a better care of the person, making them friends to water, air, light, games, sports, trips, etc.

They must be given a sincere and exact vision of an existence that is in the greatest possible accord with the biologic laws that rule the integral development of the human being.

The boys have the right to be educated with the girls and the girls with the boys, because in the social life the man does not live in a world exclusively masculine, or the woman in one exclusively feminine. Care will be taken that they do not lose the essential characteristics of their sex.

The child has a right not to be exploited by being set to work prematurely, but to be helped by the co-operation of all in furnishing him the necessities of life.

There must be formed in the child, from his earliest years, a sentiment of repulsion against the injustice and ignobility of systems for exploiting human labor.

He has the right to the co-operation of teacher and parents in his education; to the collaboration of collective society and the school, which must advance always united, constantly improving the conditions under which the school work is carried out.

He has a right to be a member of a student community where, with the autonomy which he merits, he enjoys his rights as active elements, useful and efficacious, and puts his will and abilities at the service of the common good; thus making patent at all times the value of his acts, whether they be beneficial or detrimental to himself or the community.

Children must not be judged, in any case, as common delinquents; it is necessary to clarify the influences that motivate the conduct of minors, the environment, and the living conditions to which they are or were submitted. They must not be condemned for their own misfortune. Society must search for and work towards the removal of the cause of the fault.

The duties of the child are:

To consider all companions as brothers, with equality of rights and obligations, without distinctions as to class, sex, creed, or race.

To make himself conscious of the needs of his comrades, sharing with them, as much as possible, education, food, shelter, home, and amusements.

To think, to feel and to act in search always for the well-being of the collective group, which is consequently his own; which gives the intimate satisfaction of a completed duty.

To care for his own health and to improve the conditions of public health.

To love social justice, truth and beauty and defend them with dignity and valor.

To investigate and verify the causes of natural and social phenomena without accepting dogmatic affirmations.

Exacting from all the most profound respect for the rights of the worker which our Constitution guarantees, thus, in keeping with the aspirations of the proletariat, forming juve-

nile revolutionary organizations and putting his highest qualities at the service of the wage-earning classes.

To combat idleness and vice with work and honesty, sports,
and an ethical and esthetic improvement.

To organize school co-operatives, which educate for collective production, the integral compensation of work, and the
equitable satisfaction of needs, taking care that the aspect of
individualist co-operatives be not given to these associations
where one individual is profited at the expense of the rest.

To acquit the tasks of social service efficaciously, which
his teachers and comrades of the school point out, carrying
them out by being the worker and the citizen who best serves
his family, the nation and humanity, fighting without truce,
within the limits of the Revolution, for social justice and the
disappearance of all exploitation of his equals.[18]

It thus becomes obvious that the Socialist theory of
equality is extended to include the child. The Socialists
believe that the only way in which the child will learn to
think in terms of equality is actually to live a life of
equality. He cannot be treated as an inferior by adults,
even though the adults think they are preparing the child
for a democratic life. This belief had been expressed by
John Dewey when he said, "Education is not preparation
for life; it is life." It is believed that if the child is not
exposed to domination, punishment, and regimentation as
a child, when he becomes an adult he will not think of
dominating, punishing, or regimenting others.[19] The child
is thought of primarily as a human being and secondarily
as an agent of social change. He is to be taught to think
constantly in terms of social betterment and humanity. It
is believed that too many nations put the chief emphasis of
education upon material things: money-making, subject
matter, passing examinations. Thus the focus of the school

[18] *Plan de Acción de la Escuela Primaria Socialista*, pp. 10 ff., translation by the author.
[19] Ignacio G. Tellez, *Socialización de la Cultura*, pp. 72-73.

moves off the child, and as a result the chief values the student learns are not human values:

Se considerará al niño como un agente de transformación social y como elemento real y efectivo de la comunidad en qué actua.[20]

Duties of the teacher.—Just as the school is considered by the Socialist educator of Mexico to be an instrument of social change and the child an agent of social change, so the teacher is considered a leader in social change. The teacher is not a being living an isolated existence, teaching a pure science or an academic history in a cloister. On the contrary, he must be in the midst of the social current, directing, encouraging, and, above all, leading. He is the friendly guide in the school community and in the adult world of his *pueblo, ranchería,* or city.

El maestro revolucionario debe ser líder social, consejero, orientador. No sólo debe enseñar a leer y a escribir, sino mostrar también al proletariado la manera de convivir mejor, de crear una existencia más humana y más justa.[21]

The teacher, man or woman, must stimulate the child to discover for himself new horizons of truth; but to as great an extent as possible he must let the child work out his own paths toward those truths. The teacher will point out inequalities and forms of injustice to both the school population and the adult members of society, indicating them in order to bring about their fair adjudication, however, not to stir up class hatred and unnecessary strife.[22] Self-expression and respect for the personality of the child are the keynotes that the *maestro* must strike.

[20] *Plan de Acción de la Escuela Primaria Socialista,* p. 21.

[21] Lázaro Cárdenas, speech delivered in Tlatizapan, Morelos, May 21, 1934.

[22] Emilio Portes Gil, *op. cit.,* p. 36.

The new school has regained the child's rights but wants the instructor to remember that the adult is strong and that the child is weak. The teacher's duty must be limited so the pupil can find his own ability through a process essentially spontaneous.[23]

The teacher who fits the ideal of the Mexican Socialists must be a highly practical person. He must be a better farmer than all the *campesinos* in the neighborhood, for he is court of the highest appeal in questions relating to agriculture. He must be able to guide the people to better ways of farming—deeper cultivation, fertilization, selection of seeds, and combating of pests. He must convince them that local legends and superstitious beliefs, often encouraged by village priests in the past, are untrue, and must substitute scientific facts in their stead. The teacher must lead the work of seeing that water for the villages is potable. As part of his adult education work he must teach his students to construct filters and boilers. He must take the lead in sanitation, teaching the people the theory of germs and sterilization. When people become sick he must nurse them himself or secure a doctor, seeing that local witch-doctoring is discouraged. As the first step in substituting scientific for folk beliefs he must guide the children out of the beliefs of their elders, by both precept and example.[24] He must survey the neighborhood and start longtime planning for the future exploitation of the region by the proletariat.[25]

It is the duty of the *maestro* to be so steeped in Socialist ideology that he will teach children and adults the tenets of the philosophy and lead them toward the practical application of it. This means that he must keep the people

[23] Juan B. Salazar, *Modern Educational Currents*, p. 5.
[24] *Plan de Acción de la Escuela Primaria Socialista*, p. 18.
[25] M. R. Palacios, *El Significado de la Educación Socialista*, p. 9.

struggling for the division of the large *haciendas*, according to the provisions of the Constitution, and that after the lands are distributed he must see that the people are prepared to protect them. He is a leader in the establishment of co-operatives, both productive and distributive.

A zeal matching that which sent the missionaries to the far corners of New Spain in the colonial period is today driving the Socialist school teachers over the same trails. They are advancing through the tropic jungles, over the harsh sierras, and into the arid deserts. At times they have been persecuted. During the uncertain days of the Cristero uprisings many schools were burned and the teachers were left dead or mutilated. Today they are still unsatisfied with what they have accomplished, undaunted by what remains to be done. Their goal is to rebuild the old world into the New Jerusalem, to act as midwives at the birth of the phoenix from the ashes of a dead society:

We shall educate the new generation in such a manner that we shall have men without religious prejudices, convinced of the necessity of social regulations, under which the wealth created by all will be equitably distributed; under which the instruments and means of production will be socialized; under which women will be emancipated and associated with men in working for collective progress; and under which individual perfection will be considered, not as an end, but as a means toward social perfection.[26]

[26] Rafael Ramirez, "The Six-Year Plan in Education," in *Renascent Mexico* (Covici-Friede), by Hubert Herring and Herbert Weinstock.

Chapter II

CHARACTERISTICS OF MEXICAN EDUCATION

To UNDERSTAND adequately the philosophy of the Mexican school it is necessary to examine more closely the immediate aims and goals of the system. The Mexican philosopher realizes that it is not enough to tell the *maestro* to work for a collective society but that specific techniques must be developed to meet specific situations. Mexico is a land with climate, terrain, and people so diverse that a system flexible enough to meet every local situation and not break down into a congeries of autonomous districts must have the pliability of a suit of chain mail. How is the general socialistic philosophy made to fit every situation?

MEXICAN SOCIALIST EDUCATION

The primary aim of the school is to base the entire educational structure on a foundation that is essentially Mexican. Mexican educators believe that the four hundred years of Mexican life from the Conquest onward have exhibited a constant and regrettable imitation of European customs, institutions, and habits. Many of these customs still clinging to the social fabric are as incongruous as is a Tarascan Indian saying "Ojalá," a contraction of "O Allah," when he has no idea of who Allah is. Many customs originated by the Moors have been accepted by the Spaniards and handed on to the Mexicans, for no clear reason. The school people have attempted to analyze the needs of the country, to determine the means of providing every necessity, and to teach the student to desire and work for these more functional wants:

. . . . It is a school that wants Mexico for Mexicans and that seeks to stimulate an appreciation of the value of Mexican ideas, Mexican institutions, Mexican accomplishments, and Mexican culture. It seeks to accentuate those aspects of Mexican life that give Mexico individuality and character as a nation. In short, it insists that Mexico is no longer a colonial province to be exploited at will by foreign nations and ideas, but rather that Mexico is a sovereign power with cultural attributes worthy of recognition.[1]

A word that one hears continually in present-day Mexico is "Indian." Indian is Mexico's word for proletarian. The country is predominantly Indian, and it is the aim of the present leaders to fuse the many types of Indians into a race of Mexicans. This undertaking is tremendous in the field of language alone. It is estimated that two million Indians know no Spanish whatever and that as many more know Spanish but speak some local dialect.[2] There are no data as to the number of dialects and languages spoken in Mexico, but estimates fluctuate around fifty.[3] Nahua, which is spoken in about one-third of the country, was formerly subdivided into sixteen dialects, each of which

[1] George I. Sanchez, *Mexico: A Revolution by Education* (The Viking Press, 1936), p. 104.

[2] Ernest Gruening, *Mexico and Its Heritage*, p. 86; Moisés Sáenz, "The School and Culture," *Progressive Education*, 9:9, February 1932; Luis Cabrera, "The Key to the Mexican Chaos," in *Renascent Mexico*, by Hubert Herring and Herbert Weinstock.

[3] William Gates, *Rural Education in Mexico and the Indian Problem;* Katherine M. Cook, *The House of the People*, p. 6.

was further subdivided. Yaqui is divided into Yaqui, Mayo, and Tehueco. Maya includes twenty-one dialects, of which Chañabal, Chicomucelteca, Chol, Chontal, Huaxtec, Maya, Tzental, and Tzotzil are still spoken in Mexico. The Otomí, one of the original languages, has four variants: Mazahua, Otomí, Pame, and Pirinda. The Zapotec language is used extensively in Oaxaca; Tarascan is extant in Michoacan, Totonacan in Vera Cruz, Athapascan in parts of Chihuahua and Coahuila, and Yuman and Waicurian in Baja California.

This lack of linguistic unity creates tremendous problems for the educator. He must first of all build up a desire in the Indian child to learn Spanish.[4] Señor Rivera, director of rural education in Nayarit, explained to the author the method used to teach Coras the Spanish language. When the beginners first come to the school they have no need for the language and therefore feel no desire to learn it. A group is taken to Tepic, the capital, for a day of games and sports. When they return it is easy to interest them in learning such a game as baseball. As the students play, the need for the names of objects used in the game becomes obvious. First, the name *pelota,* ball, may be learned, then bat, until gradually the children have built up a slight Spanish vocabulary. Songs and dances provide another strong motivation for an indigenous population who uniformly love movement, color, and music.[5] Under the direction of the Ethno-demographic Institute and the Cultural Missions, regional dances and songs are being collated in Spanish and furnished to the schools in all parts of the country. These methods serve the double

[4] Manuel Gamio, "Education and National Integration," *Progressive Education,* 13:2–83, February 1936.

[5] "Los Centros de Educación Indigena," *El Maestro Rural,* Julio 1937, p. 6.

purpose of unifying the people through promoting an understanding of other groups and of giving a natural impetus to the spread of the Spanish language. The Indian population of Mexico is approximately forty per cent of the total population. It ranges in culture from the Seri of Tiburón Island, in the Gulf of California, who lack even a marriage ritual, to the surviving Mayas, Zapotecs, and Aztecs, who once had a culture equal, or superior, to that of the Spaniard. The Indians' tremendous stamina and vigor is attested by the fact that they accepted the brutal exploitation and the diseases of the white man and came through to conquer him.

For the essential factor to keep in mind in understanding the present regime in Mexico is that it is the ultimate victory of the Indian. Ernest Gruening gives the following self-explanatory statistics as to the population[6] of Mexico in 1805:

Whites .... 1,000,000, equal to 18 per cent of total
Mestizos .... 2,000,000, equal to 38 per cent of total
Indians .... 2,500,000, equal to 44 per cent of total

In 1910, he reports, the relationship of the races had become:

Whites .... 1,150,000, equal to 7.5 per cent of total
Mestizos .... 8,000,000, equal to 53   per cent of total
Indians .... 6,000,000, equal to 39   per cent of total

The *mestizos* long held the unenviable position of a distinct class, unacceptable to the whites, but feeling superior to the natives. The whites played upon this class distinction in order to keep both groups in subjection. This distinction was lost during the Revolution, and the two groups are today working for class solidarity.

Educators consider it the duty of the school to teach

[6] Gruening, *Mexico and Its Heritage* (D. Appleton-Century Company), p. 69.

all members and classes of Mexico—white, *mestizo,* Indian, urban and rural—their rights and duties and to help them achieve and live up to these responsibilities. This task is tremendous because the concept of equal rights is itself almost impossible for a large part of the population to comprehend. Under the *encomienda* system in New Spain and even during the first fifty years of the republic, both State and Church considered the Indian as not being a *gente de razón,* a rational being. He was not subject to the Inquisition, and conversely he had no rights as a human being. Benito Juárez, himself a full-blooded Zapotec, was the first to lead a concerted effort to give the Indian consideration. Díaz undid his work when he abrogated the Constitution and the Reform Laws. Schools of today must therefore establish a national language and spread the doctrine of equality and respect for personality. To further this campaign *pro lengua nacional,* for a national language, teachers frequently must know the language of the locality as well as Spanish.[7] In the meantime the universal language of art, music, drama, and the dance is used to spread the Socialist doctrine. Many of the techniques used by the new schools are those used by the Church in bringing about the mental subjection of the natives during Colonial times. But the spontaneous interest of the people in the schools is a thing that the country has never known before. Today the schools are integral parts of the local communities and of the country. The school is the *casa del pueblo,* the house of the people.

Another step that educators consider necessary in the march of Mexicanization is the regaining of the economic mastery of the country. While the country has political independence, economic independence is still to be won

[7] *Programa de Educación de Acuerdo con los Postulados del Plan Sexenal,* p. 11.

by the people. In 1930 less than two thousand persons owned more than 78,000,000 hectares of land—about 195,000,000 acres, or more than one-third of the land of Mexico.[8] Foreign capital controls much of the heavy industry of the country and, as a consequence, there is the constant threat of foreign intervention. The differential[9] that exists between the Mexican and the 160,000 foreigners who either live in Mexico or control her natural resources is given in the following table in terms of pesos.

PER CAPITA WEALTH OF MEXICO

	Pesos
Mexicans	192
Foreigners in general	22,350
English	188,845
Americans	97,368
French	58,538
German	11,624
Spanish	4,185
Canadians	3,143

The program of economic Mexicanization in the schools does not aim to encourage immediate expropriation of foreign industry.[10] No more does it aim at driving out foreign ideas, such as the mechanization of industry. It aims, first of all, at making all the people conscious of the fact that the country does not belong to them and, secondly, at preparing them eventually to take over these industries and run them as efficiently as they have been run in the past. Graphic charts and tables are continually being made by the students, based on information fur-

8 M. Palacios, "El Significado de la Educación Socialista," *Progressive Education*, 12:21, February 1936; I. W. Howerth, "The Federal System of Education in Mexico," *School and Society*, September 11, 1937.

9 Gabino A. Palma, "Riqueza y Población de Mexico," *Senda Nueva*, Octubre 1935.   10 *Ibid.*

nished by the national department of education through bulletins, magazines, and lectures. These charts show the parts of the country that are owned by foreign and by Mexican capitalists. They show, for instance, the quantities of sugar that are exported and the small amount that remains in Mexico—such a small amount that many natives never have tasted the commodity. Teachers use these examples to show why the government has taken over most of the large sugar plantations and will not allow the exportation of sugar produced on government-controlled land.

Mexicanization, in the philosophy of the school, is an attempt to allow each person in Mexico to reach the point of his capabilities. He is to be freed from all inhibitions and artificial prohibitions, whether of a social, a religious, or an economic nature. The individual is to be educated to the limit of his capabilities.[11] This education is not of an academic nature but rather of an integrated, or *global*, type. The student will work toward realizing his own social rights, never, however, forgetting the rights of others. He will be a citizen of the world as well as a citizen of Mexico.

EDUCATION FUNCTIONAL, PROGRESSIVE, AND BASED ON WORK

The history of Mexico has shown that her institutions are the resultant of innumerable forces operating both from without and from within the country. So also are her schools the equilibrium of forces that have been pushing and pulling for centuries. It would be difficult to name any particular force and say, "This one made Mexico's schools functional or progressive." In 1923 a federal

[11] Joaquín Jara Díaz, "Función Social de la Educación Pública," *Revista de Educación,* Septiembre 1937.

order was sent out that all of her elementary schools were to be "schools of action." As long as the student used his hands he was considered to be progressing satisfactorily. An American, Professor Frederick Starr, introduced "functional education" to Mexico and put the schools in the progressive-education group. For a while the watchword of the country was Dewey, with his philosophy of socialization, reality, self-activity, and self-expression. According to Moisés Sáenz, former subsecretary of education, Dewey's two great services to Mexico lay in confirming Mexico's philosophy of education and in liberating her from formal school equipment.[12]

At the same time the work of a great Mexican anthropologist, Dr. Manuel Gamio, was going forward in the valley of Teotihuacán. Here he was surveying an entire segment of the national culture, a work requiring several years. On the basis of his survey he decided that only a school which embraced all the activities of the community was worth while: The individual must be integrated into the life of the group, socially, economically, politically, linguistically, and artistically.[13] This "integral education," he hoped, would guide both children and adults in all phases of their life.

. . . . "Integral education" includes guidance in diet, clothing, and shelter, in hygiene, in the methods of making a livelihood, in the relations of neighbors, in the integration of each village into the environment of which it forms a part. . . . . But to apply "integral education" intelligently it is indispensable first to study each region, since the requirements of groups living under widely diverse climatic and physiographic conditions, with differing antecedents and contacts, and in distinct stages of development, are unlike.[14]

---

[12] "Newer Aspects of Education in Mexico," *Bulletin of the Pan-American Union*, September 1929.

[13] Manuel Gamio, *loc. cit.*   [14] Ernest Gruening, *op. cit.*, p. 520.

Out of these beginnings, backed by thousands of other experiences such as the old Aztec education and the work of the early Church Fathers, grew the present-day socialistic school. The chief reason that the schools of Mexico are primarily functional is that they are largely schools for rural and proletarian population. It has been estimated that more than eighty per cent of Mexico's population is rural.[15]

Improvement of living conditions.—Because of the cultural and economic needs of the peasants, the education given in the schools is largely concerned with the problems of life on the soil or in the small community. Therefore the *maestro* is expected to live in the community and to play the leading role in all of the affairs of the place.[16] If the water supply of the region is contaminated, the teacher leads the attack upon the focus of pollution with the help of the entire community. Part of the time the students labor on their work early and join in the task. Occasionally the *maestro* explains the existence of microbes and the ways in which disease spreads. It is frequently impossible to differentiate between school and community work.

Curriculum-making thus resolves itself into a community project which soon becomes clear-cut. Teachers do not need to spend hours and days deciding what is to be taught and how it shall be taught. Needs are obvious, and the schools work to satisfy them. Perhaps the school is in

[15] Frank Tannenbaum, "The Living School," *Journal of Adult Education*, 5: 11–19, January 1933; *Programa de Educación de Acuerdo con los Postulados del Plan Sexenal* (1935, p. 13) gives 66.27 per cent. This refers to a strictly rural population, while Tannenbaum lists population in towns of less than four thousand.

[16] "Los Maestros Deben Virir en el Poblado Donde Trabajan," *Escuela Rural*, 30 de Junio, 1927; Robert J. Parker, "The Mexican School System Today," *School and Society*, 40: 558–62, October 27, 1934; Frank Tannenbaum, *Peace by Revolution*, p. 282.

a malarial or smallpox region. If so, the school provides itself with quinine or vaccinating needles. The virtue of immediate care is taught to children and adults, while gradually an attack is made on the fundamental causes of the disease. Educational work is carried forward by means of signs and posters made by the classes, who learn the life span of the malaria mosquito and the way in which it breeds and spreads disease. The posters are then placed in conspicuous places where they will add to the knowledge of the community. In the process of carrying out this specific campaign the children have read a little, written a little, drawn much, and handled the medicines and perhaps built a medicine chest. When the author visited Tepoztlan, in 1937, the school had an up-to-date medicine cabinet, made by the students and kept by them in a neat, sanitary condition. Every device known to the Department of Rural Education is at the disposal of the schools, including a weekly comic strip in one of the elementary papers for the students.[17]

Improvement of economic conditions.—Local industries, crafts, and enterprises are studied and improved. Pottery, weaving, basketry, or leatherwork may be among the sources of income of the inhabitants. If so, their techniques are studied and possible changes are made. On the Island of Janitzio part of the instruction is in *laca,* the native lacquer work on the gorgeous *jícaras* so noted in that country. In Teotihuacán the schools improved the rather crude brown and black pottery of the region, making it more serviceable but at the same time retaining the native rhythmic designs. The improved quality increased the sale of the product, considerably to the economic betterment of many of the people. Maguey fiber was devel-

[17] Polin y Pilon, *Gráfico de Agricultura,* Marzo 15, 1936.

oped in these same schools into a foundation for rug-making that now enjoys considerable vogue. Agriculture is continually studied, talked, and lived. In a country essentially agricultural it seems unbelievable that developing a school garden as an educational technique was timidly advanced by a rural teacher less than fifteen years ago. Yet such is the fact, and today garden, orchard, and aviary are almost Mexican school characteristics. Gardens are exploited in every possible form. There are experimental gardens and co-operative gardens, and gardens to provide needed vegetables for undernourished children. From time immemorial the Mexican has stirred the ground with a stick and dropped in his seed. Today it is a difficult task to convince the farmer that he should cultivate, fertilize, and irrigate. Hence on the school grounds a cornfield is often divided into several sections, to show the effects of growing maize under different conditions. In one the corn is planted and left undisturbed. In another it is weeded but not cultivated; in yet another it is weeded, cultivated, and fertilized. The results speak for themselves; and neighboring *campesinos* learn as rapidly as does the child. Various kinds of vegetables are raised in order to introduce them to the locality and encourage a better-balanced diet.

Improvement of housing.—One of Mexico's greatest social needs that is being met by the schools is a knowledge of better housing. Owing to the years of insecurity as to land tenure, the rural population has lived under miserable conditions. Fundamentally there are but two types of structures in any given locality of Mexico: the type of house used by the indigenes when the Spaniards came, and the type brought by the conquerors from Spain.[18] Often

[18] Charles Macomb Flandrau, *Viva Mexico*, p. 117; J. K. Turner, *Barbarous Mexico*, p. 111; E. D. Trowbridge, *Mexico Today and Tomorrow*, p. 110.

the homes, palaces, and churches erected by the Spaniard were impressive and ostentatious but utterly out of keeping with the locality. Materials were frequently brought from great distances and the style came even farther. A building that was ideal for the flat, arid plains of Castile would be entirely out of place in the mountains of Durango or Mexico, with their backgrounds of towering crags and their months of torrential rain. Too, their methods of construction, making use of tremendous stones of hand-hewn *tezontle* and gigantic carved beams, were entirely out of the realm of possibility for the common man. The Spaniard therefore made little or no contribution to the Mexican's knowledge of housing. The poor continued to live in the same type of house they had occupied before the Conquest.[19] In the Southeast one finds the Maya dwelling, an elliptical structure with but one opening, a door. It is ordinarily built of limestone or wattles, covered with stucco, and surmounted by a grass or palm roof. The Indians in the tropical regions still occupy thousands of *jacales,* flimsily and primitively made of palm branches. The *jacal* is often no more than a shelter, or windbreak, remaining open on one side. On the plateau there is considerable stone or adobe construction with grass or tile roofs. The tile roof is a Spanish contribution, but its use is feasible only where there is enough timber to build a strong roof frame to support the heavy tiling. In the northern and western states building has long been of adobe, with a flat roof made of closely laid willows, over which are packed several inches of earth.

When the government started its widespread rural-education program in 1921 it was confronted with the problem of housing the schools. There was so little money

[19] Robert Redfield, *Tepoztlan: A Mexican Village,* p. 31; J. Eric Thompson, *Mexico before Cortez,* pp. 95–97.

available that obviously no sort of building program could be undertaken. Therefore the policy was started, which is still being followed, of expecting the locality to furnish the school building in rural areas. Through the co-operative labor of the *campesinos* a building is erected or an abandoned structure rehabilitated. Often churches or parts of churches have been renovated and turned into schools. These buildings still show a tendency to be primitive, dark, and dirty. As these characteristics were opposed to the teachings of the new schools, it became obvious that theory and practice must be harmonized. Regional directors accordingly took a greater part in helping citizens design new structures. Later the Traveling Missions were started and took the lead in regional building. Ordinarily the Mission stays in one community for six weeks. Such a stay gives the staff time to build a model home or school from materials of the country. The design strives for more room, convenience, sanitation, and fresh air. Most of the regional normal schools have model homes which combine all these features and yet remain within the cost range of the people.

After a school has been provided, there yet remains extensive work for the teacher and pupils to accomplish. A carpenter shop and a forge are obtained, and the school community goes about its work of improving working and living conditions. If the building provided is part of an old structure, it may be floored, then windows may be cut out, and curtains may be provided by the girls in their domestic science work. Pens and cages are built and maintained for pigeons, pigs, chickens, rabbits, or whatever animals the students can obtain. A theater, either indoor or open-air, is built next. Basketball standards are erected and a court is cleared and leveled for physical activities. This practical activity does not exclude the learning of more academic subjects, for interspersed with the manual and physical activity are study periods when the students avidly read material furnished by the federal department on methods of doing all these things.[20] Blueprint and plan reading come naturally as plans are drawn and followed by the group. Most of the readers for the classes are filled with stories of children who improved their own environment; or they may include the story of a region that was visited by drought continuously until the people constructed a dam and led water, co-operatively, to the fields.[21]

In general the mornings are spent studying Spanish, arithmetic, sociology, natural sciences, agriculture, and animal husbandry. The afternoons are then devoted to the school community's needs. Afterward the students indulge in songs, dances, and games while the adults are assembling for their discussions and classes.

Campaign against alcoholism.—A campaign against *alcoholismo,* or intemperance, is sponsored by all the federal schools of the country. Drinking *pulque,* the fermented juice of the *maguey* plant, is a well-nigh national custom that dates back into the early years of the primitive peoples. Among both Mayas and Aztecs there was much imbibing of a ceremonial nature. General drinking was forbidden among the Aztecs; in fact, persons under seventy who overindulged were liable to forfeit their lives.[22] There are, however, many records of the excesses to which drinking was carried during religious orgies. Today *pulquerías* are plentiful in most parts of Mexico, and even in the states where prohibition is in effect *pulque* is in evidence. There

[20] Calso Flores Zamora, "Mexican Rural Education and Administration," *Progressive Education,* February 1936.

[21] Simiente, Libros, I, II, III, and IV; *El Pueblo Que Tenia Sed; Lecturas Populares.*

[22] J. Eric Thompson, *op. cit.,* p. 68; Leslie J. Mitchell, *The Conquest of the Maya,* p. 167.

An old-style home. Part of education's job in Mexico is to teach people to build and live in better homes.

Typical adobe home, near Monterrey

are, or course, other alcoholic beverages sold and drunk in the country, but none of them have the high consumption rate of *pulque.* The reasons for this universal thirst are manifold. Primarily, the drink is so cheap that the natives feel they cannot afford not to drink it. On the plateau a liter, slightly more than a quart, sells for less than four cents. Secondly, *pulque* drinking has been a form of national escapism during the centuries of bestial oppression.

The people of the contrey are of a good stature, tawny coloured, broad faced, flat nosed, and given much to drink both wine of Spaine and also a certeine kind of wine which they make with hony of Magueiz, and roots and other things which they use to put into the same. They call the same wine Pulco. They are soone drunke, and given to much beastliness, and void of all goodnesse.[23]

When the civil and ecclesiastical authorities had ground the last *centavo* from the peon, there was nothing left for him except a religious fiesta at which he was encouraged to imbibe to the point of oblivious drunkenness. Often the *hacendados* forced the laborers to take part of their pay in *pulque.*[24]

Pulque takes a tremendous toll from the Mexican nation from the standpoint of health, culture, and economics. The method of obtaining *pulque* is unhygienic to the highest degree: After a *maguey* plant has been topped, the *aguamiel,* honey water, which wells into the cavity is sucked out through a long gourd, the *acocote,* by the *tlachiquero.* The suction created by the *tlachiquero's* lips draws in the liquid, but also draws back saliva, thus adding to the bacteria count. The *aguamiel* is carried to the *tinacal* in pigskin containers and there placed in beef-hide vats to ferment. Various impurities are added to hurry fermentation.

[23] Richard Hakluyt, *The English Voyages* (Oxford University Press, New York), VI, 286.
[24] Frank Tannenbaum, *Peace by Revolution,* pp. 28–30.

Among the adulterants that are poured into the *pulque* are *tequesquita*, a chalky rock; *xixi*, a native plant that contains lye; vegetable parings; and sometimes even *caninilla*, or dog excrement, to increase the fermentation.[25] The distribution is equally disgusting and primitive. *Pulquerías* ladle out the liquor from open containers. The alcoholic content is about equal to that of beer, but *pulque* is a bacterial culture that continues its ferment in the intestines and may eventually lead to a toxemia causing a drunken stupor. The "national curse" is in evidence in every stratum of society. Mothers frequently wean their children on *pulque* because it can be obtained for twelve *centavos* a liter, while milk is thirty. Laborers in field and factory carry gourds or jugs of the milky fluid, which they consume as their thirst is aggravated by the heat. Church festivals are often little more than drunken orgies that frequently last two or three days.[26]

From an economic standpoint *pulque* is a parasite, sucking the lifeblood from the nation. Production and consumption of the liquor is bound up with the life of the people on the *mesa central* to such an extent that it resembles a cancerous growth that can scarcely be extracted without taking the life of the victim. Drinking other forms of alcoholic beverages in addition to *pulque* makes a burden indeed for the already hagridden country to withstand:

In 1923 taxes were paid on a production of 294,117,750 litres (litre = 1.0567 quarts). The Department of Statistics calculated that year's per capita consumption in the nine *pulque*-growing states (Hidalgo, Tlaxcala, Mexico, Puebla, Vera Cruz, Querétaro, Guanajuato, Michoacán, San Luis

[25] Ernest Gruening, *Mexico and Its Heritage* (D. Appleton-Century Co.), p. 538.

[26] Carl Lumholtz, *New Trails in Mexico*, p. 125; also Phillips Russell, *Red Tiger*, p. 281.

Potosí) and the Federal District, to be 458 litres, or one and a quarter litres daily. The consumption is undoubtedly much greater—for the large quantities consumed in the fields cannot be estimated. It greatly exceeds that of other alcoholic beverages. In the same year, the total production and importation of wines, liquors, and spirits of all kinds was given as 42,848,035 litres—also a great underestimate, since *aguardiente* in the tropics, and *mescal,* distilled from a smaller variety of agave, are made privately in many hamlets. The consumption of beer was 48,485,746 litres, an accurate figure, since it is possible to keep check on the output of breweries. Reduced to terms of alcoholic content, the National Department of Statistics calculated an annual consumption equivalent to 7.93 litres of pure alcohol per person in Mexico, compared with 4.20 in Holland and 2.31 in Norway.[27]

The schools have here undertaken a task that rivals the cleaning of the Augean stables. President Calles had to admit defeat when it came to abolition of the *pulque* industry. If the truth were known, perhaps more than one of the federal school teachers who have sacrificed their lives ostensibly to the Cristeros was a victim of a local liquor lord who resented the teacher's outspoken attacks on the evil. At least one state director lost his position from the same cause:

So dependent is the city [San Cristóbal in Chiapas] upon the sale of *aguardiente* to the Indians, and upon the exploitation of them that an attempt by the Federal School Director to initiate an anti-alcoholic campaign among the Chamula Indians led to such violent protests and difficulties (including the murder of two teachers by members of the white community), that the Director was forced to leave the State. In more than one instance, teachers who have been educating the Indians to a sense of their rights have been murdered.[28]

[27] Ernest Gruening, *op. cit.,* pp. 540–41. Statistics were taken from *Estadística Nacional,* No. 3, February 15, 1925, p. 10.

[28] Frank Tannenbaum, *Peace by Revolution* (Columbia University Press), p. 30.

Patiently the teachers are working, day after day, with the younger students in day school and the adults in night school. Murals and posters are made that show graphically the loss to worker and country from *alcoholismo*. All of these activities show that the Mexican school is attempting to develop a type of Mexican citizen superior to the Mexican of the past. The school aims to be functional and progressive through being a school of work or of action. A functional or progressive curriculum does not provide that any form of activity that teacher or student may choose to indulge in is acceptable, but that socially useful and meaningful activity only may be included. Mexico intends to train men and women to bring about social change. How successful Mexico has been in that work so far is attested by at least one American sociologist, who says, "In actual preparation for life Tepoztlan's educational methods are superior to Middletown's."[29]

MEXICAN EDUCATION FREE, OBLIGATORY, INTEGRAL,
AND DESIGNED TO ORIENT

Providing free federal schools which every child shall be compelled to attend is a part of the socialist school program of Mexico.[30] So far it seems little more than a dream, a chimera, and an observer looking at Mexico's problem would be at liberty to call it an impossibility were it not for the accomplishments to date and the aggressive way in which the government is pushing forward a system of schools that thinly covers the entire republic. There are

[29] Stuart Chase, *Mexico: A Study of Two Americas* (The Macmillan Company), p. 172.

[30] J. Jesus de la Rosa P., *La Escuela Socialista Mexicana*, p. 60; *Plan de Acción de la Escuela Primaria Socialista*, p. 7; I. G. Tellez, *Socialización de la Cultura*, p. 37.

schools in every part of Mexico, and the building of new ones goes on unabated. The author has seen the familiar *escuela rural federal* in the most unlikely and unexpected spots in Mexico, and many other observers report the same thing.[31] When, however, one looks at the other side of the picture, he wonders how soon nature will checkmate man with the tremendous obstacles she imposes. Besides the barriers of race, language, caste, and custom confronting the educational zealots, there are the geographical barriers of steaming jungle heat, of *barrancas* thousands of feet deep that contain raging, impassable rivers when one of the sudden rainstorms arises, and of mountain ranges that traverse the nation in every direction and thrust their summits up to from six to twelve and fourteen thousand feet. In places cornfields are so steep that the workers have to let each other down by ropes in order to plant and harvest their crops. Many a village varies a thousand feet in its elevation from one boundary to the other.[32] In the north and west are deserts where the *misioneros* of the present government follow trails blazed by Father Eusebio Kino and other missionaries a hundred and fifty years ago.

The only evidence that a school can ultimately be provided for every child in Mexico lies in the statistics of what has been accomplished since 1921. The evidence of the sincerity of Socialist policy over that of the *ancien régime* appears from an objective comparison. The following statistical survey[33] (p. 40) is illuminating.

[31] Ernest Gruening, *op. cit.*, p. 523; Frank Tannenbaum, *op. cit.*, chapter xxv; K. A. Sarafian, "New Schools in Old Mexico," *School and Society*, 35:890, January 16, 1932; George I. Sanchez, *Mexico: A Revolution by Education*, pp. 111–14; Larry Barretto, *Bright Mexico*, pp. 144 ff.

[32] Robert Redfield, *op. cit.*, p. 71.
[33] Manuel R. Palacios, *loc. cit.*

Year	Educational Budget (Pesos)	Percentage of National Budget
1868–1907	70,881,684.05	4.555
1907–1908	7,010,249.92	6.758
1908–1909	7,141,019.03	6.768
1909–1910	6,600,165.00	6.744
1910–1911	7,862,420.74	7.089
1911–1912	8,183,162.37	7.485
1912–1913	8,155,443.20	7.323
1913–1914	13,926,600.12	9.866
1914–1915	9,656,473.65	6.875
1917	1,507,516.29	1.212
1918	1,389,175.44	1.266
1919	1,812,693.75	.842
1920	2,218,165.75	.936
1921	12,296,265.00	4.903
1922	49,826,716.00	12.987
1923	52,362,913.50	15.026
1924	25,523,347.60	8.565
1925	21,568,575.41	7.138
1926	22,434,925.96	7.138
1927	20,036,708.83	7.035
1928	25,821,601.54	9.005
1929	27,165,063.07	9.616
1930	33,221,721.70	11.309
1931	35,200,000.00	11.753
1932	28,822,103.36	13.392
1933	31,627,289.34	14.673
1934	31,319,183.28	12.844
1935	44,450,000.00	16.153

In 1936 the amount spent was 52,065,086.57 pesos, 18.13 per cent of the total budget. The budget for 1937 was 53,862,765.83, to which later was added 1,797,679.26 pesos. It was the aim of the National Revolutionary Party and of President Lázaro Cárdenas to devote 15 per cent of the budget in 1934 to education. For 1935, 16 per cent would be earmarked for education; for 1936, 17 per cent; for 1937, 18 per cent; for 1938, 19 per cent; and for 1939, 20 per cent. During these same years it was hoped to add new schools in the following numbers: one thousand in 1934; two thousand each year from 1935 to 1938 inclusive; and three thousand in 1939. In 1929 there were 6,106 rural primary schools in Mexico; in 1933, the year before Cárdenas took office, there were 7,018; in 1936, there were 11,133 rural primary schools. Rural teachers increased in the same period as follows: in 1929 there were 7,179 rural primary teachers; in 1933 there were 9,298; and in 1936 there were 14,743.[34] Students in these same schools numbered 282,253 in 1929, 582,820 in 1933, and 737,329 in 1936. These figures do not, or course, include the urban primary schools, the secondary schools, the rural normal schools, and other normal and special schools that the government maintains.

If one looks back over its history he is likely to be pessimistic as to the future of Mexico in spite of these apparently optimistic data. The nation is such a rich pawn in the hands of exploiters that she has never been able to succeed even when she has started on a course of reform. Glancing over the table showing educational expenditures, one immediately sees that every time the budget started to climb some foreign factor crept in that flattened off the curve. When President Obregón started his idealistic work in 1921, and seemed on the way to success, he was murdered by a Cristero, a Catholic fanatic. The Cristero uprisings held the educational budgets down from 1924 to 1929. Again in 1934, the schools suffered a setback due to the Catholic Church's calling a student strike. Today the influential classes and the Church are still throwing all their weight against the advance of the schools. In self-defense the government is turning more and more to the Indian for the support of numbers and of interest. The Indian has consistently proved himself to be the best revolutionary, and is today the government's staunchest supporter.

[34] "Estadística," *Revista de Educación,* Septiembre 1937. *School and Society* (November 6, 1937) lists 11,078 schools in 1936 and 14,734 teachers.

A synthesis of all this activity would lead to the belief that the Socialist schools are making a realistic as well as an idealistic effort to live up to their aim of being free and obligatory. Yet it appears that many years must still elapse before every child will be established in a federal school and the promises of the program are completely carried out. The third characteristic within this group, "integral," signifies to the authors of the plan that the entire school system will be integrated and articulated within itself. A complete system is envisioned that will comprise education from the *jardin de niños* to a government-supported Socialist university. This plan does not include the present *universidad nacional,* which has been guaranteed autonomy by the government. While the complete plan for the final integrated system is worked out and is in operation in many urban centers right up to the university, it is still largely theoretical when considered on a nation-wide scope. The first drive of the Secretariat of Education is to see that every child is in a primary school. When that objective is attained, the next goal will be the establishment of secondary schools over the entire country.

School organization.—The *jardín de niños* is showing the same saltatory growth that has marked the spread of the primary schools. In 1934 there were 59 such centers; in 1935 the total jumped to 120; and in 1936 there were 154. The Mexican kindergarten is a social-welfare as well as an educational center. Its purpose is to help care for the children of working mothers, to add to the physical health of the child through rest, sunshine, and dietary corrections, and to start the work of socialistic indoctrination. The work is carried on through free games and activities and the use of drawing, sand tables, conversations, and trips to laboratories, factories, workshops, and the homes of workers. If the child is from a moderately well-to-do home he is to be made conscious of the conditions under which his less-fortunate brothers live. If he comes from the poorest type of home, the environment of the kindergarten is expected to arouse in him the need for a simple, economical, hygienic, moral, and aesthetic home.[35] Cleanliness, better health habits, and a knowledge of nature are stressed. Nature study is considered of prime importance because it begins the training in a rational concept of nature, makes the child conscious of the natural needs and benefits of the country, and adds to the child's collection of specific information upon which he can later build scientific generalizations. Study is made of seasonal changes, of the superficial habits of insects, birds, and animals, and of the need to conserve natural resources through the saving and planting of trees and shrubs. Patriotism is inculcated through teaching respect for the flag, from historical stories, and from trips to museums and archaeological centers of interest.

The primary schools fall into three classes: rural, semiurban, and urban. Rural primary schools are of four years' duration, while the semiurban and urban include two cycles—the four-year one and an upper cycle of two years. At the completion of the four-year rural school the student may enter the regional rural school, where he specializes in agricultural problems for two years. Those students who desire to be rural teachers may then go through the third year of school. In the cities the graduates of the four-year elementary may either enter special vocational courses or continue through the upper two years of the primary. Graduates of the six-year elementary school are

[35] Secretaria de Educación Pública, *Jardines de Niños y Escuelas Primarias*, 1937, pp. 19–25; Rosaura Zapata, "La Educación del Niño en la Edad Pre-Escolar," *Revista de Educación,* Julio 1937.

ready for the technical and vocational schools, and those of the secondary school may enter the higher technical and vocational schools, the preparatory school, or the superior normal. At the completion of the preparatory school the student is ready for the university.

The regional rural school.—The regional rural school has had an interesting evolution. During the period of the organization of the Mexican school system in the 1920's the rural normal was created. It followed the pattern of the rural primary school in that it was designed to meet the social and economic needs of the region. At the same time the Federal Secretariat of Agriculture established agricultural schools in various sections of the country. As these schools had no precedent in Mexico, they were patterned after American and European colleges. Modern machinery was introduced, pure-bred stock was purchased, and, in general, model schools of the North American type were established. From the first, these centers failed because they were not adapted to their locale. In few parts of Mexico is it feasible or desirable to use power machinery, combines, gang plows, and other large-scale farming equipment. The pure-bred stock generally succumbed to local diseases and insects. In 1932, the *Centrales Agrícolas* were turned over to the Secretariat of Education with an enrollment of approximately fifty per cent of capacity.

The agricultural schools and the rural normals were combined as rapidly as expedient into the regional training schools. This branch is under the Department of Rural Normal Schools and Cultural Missions. An education was provided that fitted each particular locality, more emphasis was placed on preparing rural teachers, and the social sciences were given equal importance with purely technical training. There were nine *Centrales Agrícolas* when they were turned over to the Secretariat of Education. The

Department had seventeen rural normal schools functioning in as many states when the agricultural centers were added. By 1934, the number of normal schools had been reduced to eleven, while there were but five agricultural schools left. The remainder had been merged to form six regional training schools. There were 901 boys and girls in these schools.[36] By the summer of 1937, all of the schools had been fused and others had been added, bringing the total to thirty regional training schools, in which 3,455 students were receiving instruction.

Instruction in the regional training school is free; that is, the government pays all of the students' living expenses. The school is expected to be a general college for the rural population. It leads the *campesino* nearer to his *capacitación* than does the rural primary. Emphasis is still placed on regional culture and on improving methods of living for the population and introducing improved techniques of agriculture and industry. The students are trained in leadership quite naturally through being leaders while they are in school. They organize co-operatives in the school and community; they have committees for all the necessary activities of the school; and all the time they take the responsibility for the success of the school.[37]

Because of the tremendous demand for teachers, practically all of the graduates of the regional training schools enter the teaching field. The ultimate aim is to have enough schools of this nature to give every child who can profit by it training in agriculture or education so that he can choose between teaching and farming. At the present time there are not even enough of these schools to meet the demand

[36] Secretaria de Educación Pública, *Memoria Relativa al Estado Que Guarda el Ramo de Educación Pública*, I, 109.

[37] "La Educación Agrícola y Normal Rural," *Conferencia Interamericana de Educación*, III, 26.

for teachers, so that a large percentage of the teachers are simply rural school graduates.

Technical and vocational education.—The Department of Technical Education is providing training in many of the skills, arts, vocations, and professions throughout the country. Their work is integrated closely with the work of the regular schools in many instances and is in separate plants in others. Technical work is offered in night schools for the students who have completed four years of elementary work and wish to complete further training. These *escuelas de artes y oficios* function as annexes to the prevocational schools that have been established in various parts of the nation. Graduates of the full six years of primary education may go into the prevocational schools, of which there were twenty-one in July 1937. Ten of these schools were located in the Federal District and the remainder were scattered over the Republic.[38] These schools aim to give immediate training for industrial and vocational participation and preparation for the vocational and professional schools. Both prevocational and vocational school courses are of two years' duration. Special technical schools have been established in conjunction with regular schools for giving vocational training to girls. Another type of school that is arousing considerable interest is the school for the children of the Army, a six-year primary school that gives special emphasis to various kinds of shopwork. The government maintains these schools, as the name indicates, for the children of soldiers. The expense of their food, shelter, and education is borne entirely by the government. There were six of these schools in 1937: two in Mexico City and one each in Patzcuaro, Guadalajára, Torreón, and Tlaxcala.

[38] Juan De Dios Batiz, "La Realización de la Enseñanza Técnica, de Conformidad con los Establecido por el Plan Sexenal," *Revista de Educación,* Julio 1937.

The secondary school.—The secondary school extends socialistic education three years upward from the sixth year of the primary school. It, too, is a unique, Mexican type of school that has been organized since the Revolution. In 1868 the *escuela preparatoria* was organized in Mexico, based on European and North American patterns. During the year of its inception there were 568 students enrolled, a select aristocratic group preparing solely for the university. Ten years later there were but 880 students in this branch of education, showing that it was not designed to meet demands for popular education. By presidential decrees of August 29 and December 22, 1925, the secondary school was established. A little more than a year later 6,563 were adolescents enrolled in secondary education. At first an enrollment fee was charged, but in 1935 the secondary school was declared gratuitous and that year saw 11,640 Mexican children of both sexes attending. Of this number 76.7 per cent belonged to the working class, 19.86 per cent to the middle class, and 3.44 per cent to the aristocracy.[39]

In view of the fact that but a small percentage of the students in the secondary school will enter the university, the curriculum has been constructed so as to be of immediate social and practical value. It continues the methods and techniques of the elementary school and attempts to deepen the student's consciousness of the country's social needs. An essential part of the secondary program is the prevocational work given in all schools. Shops are established where training is given in carpentry, metalworking, leather work, printing, domestic science, and many other practical arts. The purpose of this work is twofold: to help the student choose the type of occupation for which

[39] Juan B. Salazar, *Bases of the Socialist Secondary School* (English translation by Francisco Olave), p. 14.

he is fitted and which interests him, and to give training that will make him able to better himself vocationally.

The Socialistic Secondary School, as the prevocational institution of Mexican Society, is the kind of institution which offers real possibilities for human improvement. It is the laboratory school meant to bring forth new generations, as well as the educational establishment of modern times; an institution wherein the destinies of a better Mexico will be modeled (not a foreign colonial Mexico or industrial protectorate); but a country the natural products of which, its lands, oil, industries and woods may be directly exploited for the benefit of the laboring classes, actually working such fields of production.[40]

The characteristics of the secondary school as given by Professor Juan B. Salazar,[41] Chief of the Department of Secondary Education, are as follows:

A. It is a middle-education school.
B. It is a democratic school.
C. It socializes youth.
D. It is a selective school.
E. It gives practical instruction.
F. It builds human character, and educates for citizenship.
G. It is prevocational.
H. It combats bureaucratic intellectualism.
I. It is the school of work and social reconstruction.
J. It is a complete education.
K. It is the school of co-operation.
L. It is conspicuously social.

The aim of the Socialist secondary school is to turn out a self-reliant proletarian who will be a class-conscious workman of a high type rather than an academically trained proletarian who will join the ranks of the white-collar unemployed and who will look with contempt on the working man.[42]

[40] Juan B. Salazar, op. cit., p. 19.   [41] Ibid., pp. 13-19.
[42] Programa de Educación de Acuerdo con los Postulados del Plan Sexenal, p. 19.

One of the most noticeable features of the schools of Mexico, and particularly of the secondary school, is the amount of work done by student and teacher. It appears that they are trying to make up for the centuries of neglect in as short a time as possible. For instance, in the first year of the secondary school the curriculum demands thirty-two hours per week and in the second and third year thirty-six hours per week.

The program for the third year will serve as a sample of the instruction: Four hours a week are devoted to Spanish, with chief emphasis upon Spanish-American literature; three hours to foreign language, either English or French; two hours to civics, where consideration is given to the economic problems of the Mexican people, Revolutionary law, and agrarian and labor legislation. Economic and social geography consumes three hours weekly, while universal history considered from a materialistic standpoint is given an equal amount of time. Biology, which considers microbiology and human hygiene primarily, receives three hours weekly, as do mathematics and chemistry. At the same time the student is doing physical work of the following nature: Drawing, modeling, woodcarving, and plaster figures, two hours per week; music, one hour; physical culture, three hours; and laboratory experiments in chemistry and anatomy, two hours weekly. Every child spends four hours each week in the workshops. In addition to this stint the students form co-operatives— including farm productive and a store—for the use and education of the school. They have committees for social aid and betterment of the community and for the spread of Socialist ideology. In addition, trips are continually being made to factories, slums, and points of archaeological interest.

The spread of the secondary school has been slow and

will continue to be retarded for many years. There are several reasons for this: first of all, since there is not sufficient money to finish the work of establishing both elementary and secondary schools, the primary schools come first. Second, there will not be a tremendous demand for secondary education for a number of years because of the fact that a high percentage of the students in the primary grades are dropping out after one year in school to help out their families. As economic pressure is lessened on the heads of the families, children will be able to stay in school longer. As the graduates from the six-year elementaries become more and more numerous there will be a continuous demand for secondary schools and the government will have to meet it. The third reason for the slow expansion of the secondary school is the lack of teachers. While the primary teacher may be, and often is, barely able to read and write, it is obvious that the secondary teacher must be much better grounded in pedagogy, subject matter, and Socialist ideology.

There are today approximately 110 public secondary schools in Mexico. In addition there are many private and Protestant secondary and preparatory schools. In other places there are volunteer secondary schools, manned by teachers who donate an hour or two from other occupations daily. The author visited such a school in Patzcuaro, Michoacan, where almost a hundred youths are participating in secondary education, thanks to the public-spiritedness of a group of educated citizens. An engineering student, staying out of the university for a year to work, teaches engineering drawing, and mathematics; an Englishwoman living in the town teaches English; and so on through the faculty. Classes are held in the elementary school plant during the day and evening, classes being given at the hour the teacher can take off from his regu-

Many private schools are functioning under government supervision. This large preparatory school, Ateneo de la Fuente, is in Saltillo, Coahuila.

Common to all parts of Mexico is the school in an old church building. Tepoztlan.

Typical of the new Mexican school that hopes to "redeem the proletariat."

lar occupation. It is from beginnings such as these that Mexico works toward the day when there will be free, obligatory secondary education over all the nation: "Compulsory education on the secondary level is one of our greatest pedagogical objectives."[43]

MEXICAN SCHOOLS COEDUCATIONAL

Coeducation is a strange, new concept in Mexico. For a few years it caused an issue over which the nation ranged itself in two camps. On the one side stood the Socialists and the moderns clamoring for coeducation in all the schools, saying that the only training for social life comes from the two sexes mingling while they are in school. On the other side stood the clergy, the religious, and the conservatives, saying that coeducation leads to immorality and lasciviousness. The battle reached its crux in 1935, and since then the anticoeducational camp has become less vociferous if not more reconciled.

The federal rural and elementary schools quite naturally fell into a coeducational pattern called *escuelas mixtas,* or mixed schools. When, however, the effort was made to extend coeducation upward, the real fight began. The cream of Mexico's secondary schools are in Mexico City. When they were established, they were definitely for boys or for girls. In 1936, they became coeducational. Some teachers seated all the boys on one side and all the girls on the other; others seated them alphabetically without regard to sex. Everyone was very conscious of the fact that classes were mixed, however, and the situation was distinctly humorous to an American. But by 1937 coeducation was already being taken as a matter of course and

---

[43] Enrique Beltran, "The Place of the Biological Sciences in Education Programs," *Progressive Education,* February 1936.

teachers were concerning themselves with more important problems. At the same time that the secondary schools were made coeducational, the different grades of the technical and vocational schools opened their doors to both sexes.[44]

Mexico has the weight of both Indian and Spanish tradition against equality of sexes. In ancient Aztec and Mayan days the two sexes were segregated almost completely before marriage; they were educated separately, and marriage was arranged by the parents.[45] The Moorish customs followed by the Spaniards in regard to the practical seclusion of women are too well known to need recapitulation. In spite of this cultural lag, the Socialist ideology calls for equality of the sexes, legally, educationally, socially, and economically.

Mexican educators believe that they must prepare the secondary students for coeducation through elementary mixed schools. When the adolescent period is reached, they feel, especial guidance must be given the students so that the boys, who they feel have a stronger biological urge than girls, will not debase their female companions. They also feel that great care must be exercised so that education will be adapted to both sexes and will not be solely masculine. They place considerable emphasis on the fact that they expect the girl to maintain her womanly characteristics and not to be hardened so that she acquires masculine patterns.

. . . . with regard to *moral order* coeducation teaches both respect and gentleness towards women who become bet-

[44] Miguel Huerta, "La Politécnica Abre Sus Puertas a la Mujer," *Senda Nueva*, Octubre 1935; "La Coeducación en las Escuelas Post-Primarias," *Senda Nueva*, Diciembre 1936.

[45] J. Eric Thompson, *Mexico before Cortez*, pp. 45 ff; Frans Blom, *The Conquest of Yucatan*, chapter xxi; E. L. Hewett, *Ancient Life in Mexico and Central America, passim.*

ter prepared for the *Sex Struggle*. As for the physiological order, it is the natural soothing remedy for sexual desires, and the best preparer for the reciprocal knowledge of qualities and deficiencies of the sexes. In connection with the *social economic order,* coeducation will enable woman to follow any profession or business activity that she can perform as well as any man; thus enjoying moral independence, instead of the old-fashioned slavery into which she was formerly dragged.[46]

MEXICAN EDUCATION CO-OPERATIVE AND EMANCIPATORY

One of the important goals of Mexican education is training for a collective society. In this society property is not necessarily held in common, but work will be done co-operatively and the final aim of every activity is the common good. Citizens are to learn to work together for their mutual benefit, not to think of other human beings as units to be exploited for the aggrandizement of a few.

For this reason the schools emphasize co-operation in all its phases. There is a co-operative store in every school that has the attendance to support one. There are co-operative gardens, where the students work together and share the profits. But, above all, the school organization is co-operative. Community, students, and faculty share equally in the management of the school. Teachers have an equal voice with educational authorities in the choice of a director of the school. Students may cause the removal of any teacher they do not approve. Students and teachers soon learn to work together and respect each other, thus educating for equality of rights and respect for personality.

While the Mexican has long been used to communal organization, he is still primarily an individualist. In the *ejidal* distribution of land the village has its commons; but each citizen has his own individual plot which he and his family work. Thus the group members do not work

[46] Juan B. Salazar, *Bases of the Socialist Secondary School,* pp. 26 f.

co-operatively; they work individually on lands held in common. In the past a large part of the work of the country, such as farming, spinning, weaving, and handicrafts of all sorts, has been individual. Political and social organizations have never been extensive and well articulated. The history of the country shows extensive use being made of *caciquismo*—holding one chief or *cacique* responsible for keeping his group in order and collecting the taxes. This *cacique* was usually venal, exploiting his group as mercilessly as would any Spaniard. Antonio de Mendoza, first of the viceroys to New Spain, left a letter of advice to his successor, Luis de Velasco, in which he warned him of the cruelty of minor Indian officials to their own people. The *calpisques* or native overseers had a reputation for harsh treatment of their countrymen, while their *caciques* had to be watched to prevent them from robbing their own people.[47] As a result the schools are facing the task of undoing the social conditioning of centuries.

Every phase of the school work stresses social co-operation. There is as little formal, individual recitation and examination as possible. Class work is essentially training in group participation; class projects and group endeavors are paramount. Sports are for group participation as much as possible, with the team idea uppermost. Regional dances are used for the same reason; they have a tendency to develop a sense of solidarity, an esprit de corps among the students.

The emancipatory characteristic of Mexican education is one that ramifies into the other activities and characteristics. Mexican education expects to emancipate the *paisano* from economic slavery by teaching him co-operative organization and encouraging the formation of confedera-

---

[47] L. B. Simpson, *The Encomienda in New Spain,* pp. 185 f.

tions, guilds, unions, and leagues. It expects to emancipate him from land poverty by teaching him his constitutional rights, according to the actual provisions of the constitution, so that he will know that he is entitled to land and will demand that it be given him. Mexican education expects to emancipate the people from fanaticism and superstition, giving them instead a rationalistic and scientific view of the universe.

Chapter III

FURTHER CHARACTERISTICS OF MEXICAN EDUCATION

To ARRIVE at an exact understanding of Mexico's stand toward religion, and to see clearly the part the school plays in the Church-State controversy, the student must thread a careful way through a labyrinth of conflicting statements, historical data, and modern dogma. When he has done these things and has studied the schools in action he finds clearly that Mexican education is not against any honest religion, nor is it against religious teaching.[1] Mexican education, however, declares itself against superstition, fanaticism, bigotry, and religious exploitation. The purpose of this chapter is to find how this statement squares with the fact that the Catholic Church has been forced to close its schools and cut down the number of its clergy in Mexico in 1935 from 4,493 to less than 300. A glance at Article 3 of the Constitution shows that the major emphasis is placed on an education that, "excluding all religious doctrine, shall combat fanaticism and prejudices by organizing its instruction and activities in a way that shall permit the

---

[1] C. Trejo Lerdo de Tejada, *La Educación Socialista*, chapter iv; J. Jesús de la Rosa, *La Escuela Socialista Mexicana*, p. 68; "Combatir el Fanatismo no es Atacar Credos Religiosos," from a speech by President Cárdenas in *El Maestro Rural*, 15 de Marzo, 1936.

creation in youth of an exact and rational concept of the Universe and of social life."[2] Former President Emilio Portes Gil elucidates this section rather clearly in a few paragraphs:

In the first place it gives to the teaching rationalist (*racionalista*) orientation with the purpose that the school shall accustom the pupils to explain scientifically the phenomena of nature. The carrying out of this object imposes upon those charged with imparting knowledge the duty of freeing the minds of the pupils from the prejudices which, as a social inheritance from past generations, have been conserved as an arbitrary explanation of the phenomena of the Universe and are without any scientific basis.

The second object of the reform tends to create in children sentiments and ideas of human fraternity, and moral and economic rehabilitation of the society of today, in order that they may learn to correct the irritating inequalities at present existing in Mexico, according to the provisions of the Revolutionary laws of the country and practically through the dispositions of Article 27 and 123 of the General Constitution of the Republic.

The establishment of the Socialistic school in Mexico depends upon the social and peculiar ideals of the Revolutionary movement, which has endeavored to care for the necessities of the present social life in Mexico. *The reform of Article 3 does not contain any atheistic propositions.* The practice of religion is left to the religions, all of whom are officially authorized by the general constitution.

But the reform of Article 3 implies the necessity of combating prejudices and falsities which have been transmitted from generation to generation, fostering the ignorance of our humble classes so that conscienceless people may exploit them inhumanly.[3]

[2] H. N. Branch (translator), *The Mexican Constitution of 1917 Compared with the Constitution of 1857* (Supplement to *The Annals of the American Academy of Political and Social Science*, May 1917).

[3] C. S. MacFarland, *Chaos in Mexico* (Harper & Brothers), pp. 70 f.

MEXICAN EDUCATION SCIENTIFIC AND RATIONALISTIC

In a study of religion in Mexico all statements refer to the Roman Catholic Church because of the simple fact that religion in Mexico is and has been Catholic from the coming of the Spaniard until today. Another postulate of the entire problem is that the Mexican Catholic Church is not comparable to the American Catholic Church or the European Catholic Church of today. The Mexican Church was, until its almost complete emasculation by the government, largely an economic and political organization.[4] Mexican philosophers say it did not produce a body of Christians with monotheistic beliefs, did not give moral and spiritual direction to the people. After four hundred years of Catholicism in Mexico the country is declared to be saturated with superstition, fanaticism, and ignorance and nearing the vanishing point in social morals.[5] The historical development of religion in Mexico shows that the people have maintained their paganism and have lost their strict moral codes during the past four hundred years.

Pagan predecessor of the Catholic Church in Mexico.— The religion of the ancient Mexican is difficult to evaluate because of the lack of unbiased historical accounts. Early Church leaders destroyed every code and manuscript that fell into their hands. Juan de Zumarraga, first Archbishop, burned all of the beautiful native manuscripts that could be found in Mexico in one great holocaust. Later Church writers simply aimed to place the native religion in as poor a light as possible, with little regard for accuracy. Yet a very few aspects of the old religion may be listed.

Gods of agriculture formed the majority of the super-

[4] George I. Sanchez, *Mexico: A Revolution by Education*, p. 166; Moisés Sáenz and H. I. Priestly, *Some Mexican Problems*, p. 158; R. N. McLean, *That Mexican*, p. 65; C. S. MacFarland, *op. cit.*, p. 63.
[5] Ernest Gruening, *Mexico and Its Heritage*, pp. 254 ff.; Anita Brenner, *Idols behind Altars* (Harcourt, Brace & Co.), chapter vii.

natural horde, because the autochthons were primarily an agricultural people. These supernatural beings fell into three classes: gods of rain, gods of growing things, and gods of the soil. The Tlalocs were an important group among the gods of the elements, for they were mountain gods and ruled the rains, thunder, lightning, snow, rivers, lakes, and wells. Five festivals yearly were dedicated to the worship of the Tlalocs, three of which were intercessions for rain in the planting season and for the young maize.

Worship of the sun, moon, and stars was important among the primitives, Tonatiuh, the sun god, being one of the principal deities. As he gained strength by drawing moisture from the soil, the sacrifice of victims was primarily for his benefit. He needed a continual supply of human beings to help him in his journey across the heavens; hence the warriors captured in battle and sacrificed to him added strength for his labors. Women who died in childbirth also were blessed, for they were added to his retinue. There were other gods of the underworld, such as Mictlantecutli and his wife Mictecaciuatl. They ruled Mictlan, a not unpleasant place where the souls ended a four-year wandering after death. Both of these gods were symbolized by skulls or portions of skeletons. Strong vestiges of this worship are to be found in many fiestas of present-day Mexico, particularly the Day of the Dead, in which gaiety abounds in the midst of dancing skeletons. Huitzilopochtli was god of war and of the hunt. Among the Aztec nobility he was held in the greatest esteem; his temple in Tenochtitlan, the present Mexico City, was the largest and most important shrine in Mexico. He is pictured in a dress of hummingbird feathers, carrying a shield, spear, and spear thrower. Quetzalcoatl, another of the leading deities of pre-Cortesian Mexico, is indirectly credited with the downfall of the Aztec empire. His name means "Quetzal-snake," and he was supposed to be a white god with a long beard. He was shown decked out in the feathers of the quetzal bird, an exotic creature found near the Guatemalan-Mexican border. Chief center of the worship of Quetzalcoatl was at Cholula, although adjacent to the pyramid of the sun at San Juan Teotihuacan there is an extensive temple to Quetzalcoatl. His worship was further identified by the serpents' heads that were used in decorations in his temples. Quetzalcoatl was supposed to have been driven from the country, and he vengefully promised to return from the east with his followers and retake the country. Since he wore a cross on his clothing, was reputedly white, and had a beard, the legend concerning him contributed wonderfully to the prestige of the Spaniards when they arrived in 1519.[6]

When the Catholic clergy started the work of converting the Indians to the new faith, they apparently had wonderful success. Instances are recorded of one padre baptizing thousands of natives daily. There was little outward hostility to the new faith, for the reason that the native Mexican was accustomed to accept the religion of the conqueror along with his government. However, he was not accustomed to dropping his own faith; he merely added new gods to his own pantheon. In the outward forms of worship there were many similarities between Mexican paganism and Spanish Catholicism. The natives already understood and practiced the use of incense, holy oils and waters, penitence, fasting, and confession; and they carried charms, amulets, and scapularies. However, since they did not understand the theory of a single su-

[6] For more detailed information regarding primitive Mexican religion, see J. Eric Thompson, *The Civilization of the Mayas;* Lucien Biart, *The Aztecs: Their History, Manners and Customs;* and J. Leslie Mitchell, *The Conquest of the Maya.*

preme power, it is believed by Mexican materialists that they did not understand anything of the abstraction the Church attempted to teach.

A pantheistic people, accustomed to see a god in every hill, cloud, river, and tree, they had no difficulty in accepting the church or cathedral as another hallowed spot. The race, the nation, is profoundly religious. It worships also in Catholic churches. Whether or no it can be considered a creature of the Church, only the Church can answer. Often it has been doubted, but never fully questioned. Travellers and historians almost unanimously are skeptical; friars and priests voice bitterly frustration. Fray Bartolomé and Father Sahagun immediately after the conquest; Fray Jacinto de la Serna and his colleagues in the "investigation against idolaters" a hundred years later; Baron von Humboldt in the nineteenth century; Lumholtz recently, and other ethnologists today, record similarly the thing that is written in the faces of lonely rural priests. And nearly anyone in Mexico can add one episode of an idol behind a cross.[7]

The first work undertaken by the Church in New Spain was the eradication of every phase of the pagan faith. Teocallis were pulled down, codices were publicly burned, and every idol and *tepozton* found was destroyed. The people, however, hid their images in every conceivable place. Not the least ingenious concealment was contrived by the native masons, who sealed up local or regional idols in the altars of the churches or in their walls and foundations. Dozens of instances are on record of the finding of these images when altars needed repairs or when walls cracked.

In locations that were sacred to powerful Indian gods, the Fathers erected new places of worship upon the foundation of the razed teocalli. The Cathedral of Mexico City,

[7] Anita Brenner, *Idols behind Altars* (Harcourt, Brace & Co.), p. 128; see also R. N. McLean, *op. cit.*, p. 36, and Erna Fergusson, *Fiesta in Mexico, passim.*

Huitzilopochtli, is standing on the site of the great teocalli; a chuch rests atop the pyramid to Quetzalcoatl in Cholula —a pile so tremendous the Spaniards could not raze it, for it exceeds the pyramid of Cheops in volume. As Cholula was the Mecca of the Indians, an attempt was made to erect a church on the site of each temple in the city; and more than three hundred churches in a town of five thousand persons today stand as a mute reminder of this game of ecclesiastical checkers. At Tepoztlan centered the worship of Tepoztecatl, a god of such importance that pilgrims came from as far away as Chiapas to worship. The spiritual welfare of this region was entrusted to a Dominican, Father Domingo de la Anunciacion. Tepoztecatl sat majectically upon a crag overlooking the town, and the Dominican made a pact with the townspeople that the god should be pushed over the edge and if he survived the fall should be considered divine; if, however, he shattered, his worship was to be abandoned. The image broke into fragments and the masons incorporated the pieces in the foundations of the monastery that was completed in 1588.[8]

Popular festivals attracted thousands of native worshipers to certain sacred spots made holy by legends of miraculous happenings. As a Catholic holy day may be found for practically any day in the year, a Saint's day was easily substituted for that of the idol. Generally some miraculous happening was incident to the appearance of the Saint's image in the new location. Thus the Señor de Chalma suddenly appeared in the grotto of Ostotocteotl, the god of the caves, cast down the idol, and erected himself, where his worship has continued with undiminished popularity.[9] Undoubtedly the greatest case of substitution

[8] Robert Redfield, *Tepoztlan, A Mexican Village*, pp. 27 f.

[9] Erna Fergusson, *op. cit.*, chapter iii; Stanton Davis Kirkham, *Mexican Trails*, p. 126.

in Mexico is that of the Miraculous Virgin of Guadalupe. The early Church found that it could not break the worship of Topantzin, mother of the gods and special goddess of earth and corn. Her worship centered at the hill of Tepeyac, a short distance from Mexico City. Here, on the twelfth of December, came Indians by the thousand to worship and perform their ritual dances. One December day, it is related, Juan Diego, a poor Indian, came to Archbishop Zumarraga with the story that the Virgin had appeared to him on the hill and asked that a shrine be erected to her. The Archbishop doubted and asked him to bring proof of the authenticity of the tale. On the twelfth of December, oddly enough, the Virgin again appeared to Juan and plucked blooming roses from the barren, rocky hillside. When she placed them in Diego's *tilma*, her picture suddenly appeared in lustrous colors on the crude weave of the cloth. By decree of Pope Benedict XIV, this miracle was officially recognized by the Church and her shrine has since become the greatest center of worship in Mexico. Today the Indians and *mestizos* come by the thousands and again dance their pagan ritual dances, flagellate themselves, buy holy relics, have images blessed, and end with a drunken orgy.

Once a year ragtail and caballero, harlot and housewife, thief and honest man, swirl through the iron grill of the atrium, into the cathedral, around the slippery stones of the holy well, beneath the horse-shoe façade of the Capilla del Cerrito. Poor and rich, they are holy and hilarious. Awe and jest clash in a dozen dialects—Otomí, Tarascan, Aztec, Zapotec, Huastecan, and all their variants. This is Mexico's greatest fiesta. Guadalupe is still the hub of the Mexican religious wheel. Its spokes are Tlaloc and Tonantzín; Guadalupe, Moctezuma and the Pope; high mass and feather-decked dancing; holy-water and deer-eyes. Guadalupe is the religious capital of Mexico.[10]

[10] Carleton Beals, *Mexican Maze* (J. B. Lippincott Company), p. 69.

During the Revolution of 1810, the rebels carried the image of the Virgen de Guadalupe, which virgin was tried by the Church and burned while the Spanish forces fought under the aegis of the Virgen de Soledad.

Miracles and superstitions of the Catholic Church.— Once the Church was established in New Spain she did not seek to rid the people of superstitious beliefs, say the anti-clericals:

> The clerical control over the Indians is based on their superstition. Instead of propagating the religion of love, the clergy has inculcated or permitted the retention of a religion of fear, a survival of both the gloomy theology of sixteenth century Spain and the sombre Aztec terror of the unknown. The persistence of the Anáhuac spirit is visible in the extreme bloodiness of the Mexican images of the Savior.[11]

The padres reported miracles with the dawning of each day. Every natural phenomenon that occurred was a miracle or a curse. If the year were exceptionally dry, that was because of God's displeasure, aroused perhaps because the offerings had not been heavy enough. Did exceptionally heavy rains fall, it was through God's divine grace, and the people were expected to give especially heavy alms in repayment. If the Aztecs were threatened with a plague of locusts, they gathered some of the insects, crushed them in water, had incantations performed over them, and set them at the limits of the fields. The Catholic clergy took over this function and, for a fee, blessed the same concoction, which was placed as it had formerly been at the extremities of the field to rid them of the pest.[12]

Juan Obrigon, a simple native of Baja California, tells in his autobiography of a legend sponsored by the Church:

[11] Ernest Gruening, *Mexico and Its Heritage* (D. Appleton-Century Company), p. 256.

[12] Frederick Starr, *Notes upon the Ethnography of Southern Mexico, passim.*

The priests of the southern end of Baja California forbade the people to dig cellars, holes, or tunnels because of the fancied existence of a giant gopher, *La Topa Chisera*, that had diabolical powers. "Once in so often he pierced our *zanja* walls, and we who cower in our huts hear a thundering rush of water, which tears out yards of ditch and destroys acres of our best land. Should any go out at night, or without a padre, to repair our ditch, he who first places foot in the mire is pulled down into a great cavern, where this devil sits smiling and hungry for men's souls and bodies."[13]

A student at the Agricultural College in Chapingo told me that the priests in his district warned the people that if metal passed through the ground nothing would grow, thus discouraging the use of steel plows. The anticleric account goes on to state:

It was difficult in any case to say where native sorcery and religious habit ended and divine intervention that could be endorsed by the Church, began. By encouraging devotion to miraculously appeared Christs and by preaching, as must have been done, with texts of the miracles of saints and madonnas, the missionaries sowed luxuriant crops. Many more miracles occurred than the friars were prepared to admit.[14]

There is little of the necessity for the spiritual or the moral about Mexican miracles. It is not necessary that one be pious to merit divine interposition. No; the one requisite of a Mexican miracle is that it happen opportunely. There was, for an instance, the faithless wife who was surprised in the woods with her lover by her irate husband. The husband had a machete and was in a position to commit mayhem when the woman called on Our Lord of Chalma. Immediately the lover was turned into

[13] Antonio de Fierro Blanco, *The Journey of the Flame*, pp. 19 ff.

[14] Anita Brenner, *Idols behind Altars* (Harcourt, Brace & Co.), p. 158.

an altar with Christ upon it. The husband dropped machete and intentions and fell upon his knees as he and his wife worshiped.

Thieves and murderers have their own patron saints and invoke their benediction before any projected crime. If the deed is successful, they duly bring their contribution to the chapel of the saint. José de Leon Toral, murderer of President Alvaro Obregón, received the sacrament from Mother Conchita, Superior of an outlawed convent, before committing the assassination.

Mexican educators feel that so thoroughly imbued have the Mexicans become with the belief in miracles that they have little discrimination left, believing anything that is told them about sickness, death, or other natural phenomena. The average Mexican is not concerned over the high infant-mortality rate of Mexico, higher than that of China even, because they still have vestiges of the pagan belief in Tonantzin to whom the child-dead were dedicated. The Feast of the Little Dead is celebrated happily, with feasting and drinking, with the full sanction of the Church. *Ex votos* are in evidence in any church in Mexico for the visitor to see. Here the petitioner writes a postcard to God, either reciting a miracle that has happened or asking for one in the future. Some are in the nature of contracts and cannily set forth the terms : this is to be done by the Deity and in return the petitioner will pay a specified amount.

Polytheism in the Mexican Catholic Church.—Another attribute of Mexican Catholicism that has come from the combination of paganism and the medieval church is the belief in a multiplicity of gods and idols. Just as every family had its own lares and penates and every village its particular gods, so a belief in the special efficacy of certain churches and saints over others grew up. The concept

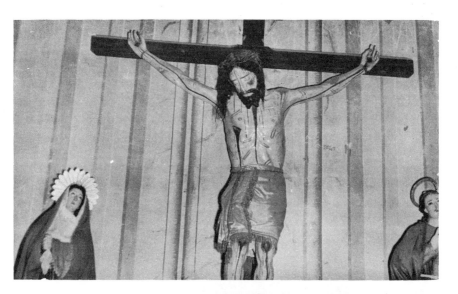

An example of the gory images of Christ that fill Mexico's churches.

Mexico's federal school men object to this sort of image. "Cristo" in church at Tepoztlan.

of Christ or God as a disembodied demiurge is unknown except to a few cosmopolite Mexicans of the cities. The Mexican enjoys a form of hagiolatry and Mariolatry of the most intense sort. Tourists who write of the tremendous spiritual experiences enjoyed by these people in the churches and cathedrals of Mexico would be surprised to know that they are probably caused by the object directly in front of the worshiper, the *santo* or the *cristo* or the *virgen*. Every church of any pretensions has its own images, the patron saint of the church, and one or more virgins and Christs, the number depending upon the size of the church.

Most of the *santos* receive veneration only in the locality. But when legends such as this cluster thickly, the image comes to be sought by people not of the region, and in this way develop the sacred shrines of Mexico, such as Guadalupe and Chalma . . . .

The word *Santo* is special and exact; there is no substitute for it, and it is used in both Spanish and Nahuatl discourse. Generally it means any sacred effigy; specifically and commonly it refers to the images of Christian saints housed in temples.[15]

Occasionally there will be a frankly pagan image which the priest and the people of today do not recognize. Gruening reports an image to the god Tlaloc in the churchyard of Milpa Alta. The author found a Toltec animal-god in the Church at San Antonio Teoloyucan standing next to a life-sized Saint John. When the priest was questioned as to its significance he looked vague and murmured, "It is of the village." Each Virgin, each Christ, each saint pictured in murals, on the walls, or carved in wood is an individual. The image represents Christ as its woodcarver or artist personally pictured him, and thus he has been

[15] Robert Redfield, *Tepoztlan, a Mexican Village* (University of Chicago Press), pp. 196–97.

perpetuated for hundreds of thousands of others according to the number that have worshiped him.

The most potent images, according to the native belief, are the dark ones, the Indian images. White Christs and Virgins are too cold and aloof. They are for the foreigners. The first Christ carved and placed in America is a white Christ found in the church of San Francisco de Tlascala. It is a grisly figure, naked, blood-splattered, having a rope about its neck. A later Christ in the same church is a dark Christ, nearly black, having a crown of thorns and a brief Indian skirt. The Christ at Tepoztlan is of the southern Indian type, slight, almost Oriental in appearance. This figure is interesting in that the left arm is shown as broken and pulled back over the arm of the cross. It is dressed in long trousers and has a skull cap. At Milpa Alta is to be found a recumbent *enceinte* Virgin in Indian dress and shod in *guaraches*. A Mexican nearly always worships at his favorite *santo*'s shrine or altar. In the large churches in Mexico, if one watches the worshipers enter, he will notice that each one goes purposefully toward one of the many altars or images and kneels in front of that one. When villagers from two or three centers of population congregate, there are arguments and fights as to whose Christ is the most potent. Certain of the saints and *Cristos* have special virtues, such as the ability to cure disease or to remove blemishes. At the fiestas, which are in session in one *población* or another all of the time, a tremendous business is carried forward in charms, trinkets that have been blessed, and miniature saints. The rationalists therefore say that the people as a whole have no idea of the meaning of Christianity. Just as in the civil governments at the time of the Conquest the people merely changed masters, so in their religion they have merely exchanged one form of idolatry for another.

The amorality of the Mexican Church.—In reviewing the charges that have been made against the Church for a lack of moral guidance, only the effects upon the people themselves will be considered. Modern Mexican school men bring serious, almost unbelievable charges against the morality of the religious of the Catholic Church. These charges they document endlessly, not least from high churchmen who periodically demanded that the money-lenders be driven from the temples. Rationalist leaders consider that the life demanded of the clergy, celibacy particularly, is scientifically and psychologically unsound and that it can lead only to depravity and certainly not to moral wardship. Discounting this phase of the situation entirely, only the statements that the Church, after having the spiritual and moral guardianship of the Mexican people in its keeping for four hundred years, has produced a people who divorce morality and religion in their thinking, whose rate of illegitimacy is high, and who have vague ideas as to temperance, chastity, and marital probity will be considered.

Under the Aztecs a moral tone was maintained that was Spartan in its severity. The Mayas and the other leading racial groups had equally high standards.

Incorrigible children might be sold into slavery as a last resort. Children, who were too prone to lie, were punished by having a piece cut out of one of their lips. With such strict training it is not strange that the Spaniards were astonished at the high moral tone of the natives, and their reluctance to tell a lie. Unfortunately contact between the two civilizations soon led to a rapid moral degeneration of the native code.[16]

An unfaithful Aztec wife and her seducer had their heads crushed with a stone dropped by the outraged husband.

[16] J. Eric Thompson, *Mexico before Cortez* (Charles Scribner's Sons), p. 40.

Drunkenness was forbidden and violators of the tabu were put to death. The *Conquistadores* started the debauchery of native morals by their indiscriminate taking of women. Under their domination native women were forced to submit to their wishes at any time. Afterward, under the *encomienda* system, the *hacendados* and their overseers exercised a species of seignorial rights over the women. This practice was continued through the days of the viceroyalty, and became more pronounced under Díaz when the rights of the owners over their peons extended to life and death.

The utmost excesses have been practiced by all classes of Mexicans, while they and the Church considered these same Mexicans to be devout members of the Church.

Of the moral code which the church should have instilled and does instill in the United States or in Catholic France there are few vestiges in Mexico. Male conjugal fidelity among the Mexican upper classes is rare. Infidelity is flagrant and reputable. Mexicans speak without restraint of their children and their "natural children." . . . . Among the masses drunkenness and sexual debauchery form the aftermath of many religious festivals, and always have. . . . . Intoxication is an invariable feature of Guadalupe Day, December 12, as anyone who has witnessed the ceremonies, as I have, can testify.[17]

One of the church customs that has helped drive the Mexican to immorality is that of placing a high charge upon such services as marriage and baptism. In the past only the church blessing was recognized; yet a high percentage of the people remained unblessed in their unions and in the fruits thereof. One of the famous passages in literary Mexicana is that of Flandrau in describing Mexico in 1908:

[17] Ernest Gruening, *Mexico and Its Heritage* (D. Appleton-Century Company), pp. 250–51.

It strikes one as strange, as wicked even, that a powerful Church (a Church, moreover, that regards marriage as a sacrament) should deliberately place insuperable obstacles in the path of persons who for the time being, at least, have every desire to tread the straight and narrow path. This, to its shame, the Church of Mexico does.

The only legally valid marriage ceremony in Mexico is the civil ceremony, but to a Mexican peon the civil ceremony means nothing whatever; he can't grasp its significance, and there is nothing in the prosaic, businesslike proceeding to touch his heart and stir his imagination. The only ceremony he recognizes is one conducted by a priest in a church. When he is married by a priest he believes himself to be married—which for moral and spiritual purposes is just as valuable as if he actually were. One would suppose that the Church would recognize this and encourage unions of more or less stability by making marriage inexpensive and easy. If it had the slightest desire to elevate the lower classes in Mexico from their frankly bestial attitude toward the marital relation—to inculcate ideas different and finer than those maintained by their chickens and their pigs—it could long since easily have done so. But quite simply it has no such desire. In the morality of the masses it shows no interest. For performing the marriage ceremony it charges much more than poor people can pay without going into debt. Now and then they go into debt; more often they dispense with the ceremony. On my ranch, for instance, very few of the "married" people were married.[18]

Dr. George I. Sanchez, himself a Catholic and an authority on Mexico, says:

For our purpose it is best to eliminate any consideration of religious doctrines or beliefs in order that we may be in a better position to judge the effects that the Church-State controversy has had on education in Mexico. I say this because of a firm conviction that religion, as such, is probably the most insignificant factor in the controversy. The conflict in Mexico has arisen because, unlike the American Church, which is

[18] C. M. Flandrau, *Viva Mexico*, pp. 91 f.

modern and in which religion is the chief concern, the Mexican Catholic Church is the medieval Church, the colonial Church, which exercised not only a religious function but a political one in which economic power was essential to its existence.[19]

It is charged that because of their conscienceless greed the votaries of the church often appear in a highly unfavorable light when an occasion arises where the people want leadership in their spiritual wanderings. Priests in Mexico have long been charged with heartless, ruthless, undignified plundering of the people in their moments of emotional weakness.

Another fertile field for wealth which the Church did not neglect was found in the fees for funerals, weddings and christenings. The charges for such services were graduated to fit individual cases, but were always as much as the traffic would bear.[20]

Let us examine these spiritual catharses as they were seen by eyewitnesses and find their nature.

Then, combining, in a quite wonderful fashion, extreme rapidity with an air of ecclesiastical calm, he made his confirmatory way down one side of the nave, across the end, and up the other, preceded by one priest and followed by two. The first gathered up the certificates (no laying on of hands unless one has paid one's twenty-five centavos) and read the name of the child next in line to the bishop, who murmured the appropriate formula, made a tiny sign of the cross on a tiny forehead with the end of a large, dirty thumb, and moved on. The second, with a bit of absorbent cotton dipped in oil, swabbed the spot on which the cross had been signed, while the third, taking advantage of the general rapture, gently relieved everyone of his blessed candle (it had never been lighted) and carried it away to be sold again.

[19] George I. Sanchez, *Mexico: A Revolution by Education* (The Viking Press, 1936), p. 166.

[20] R. N. McLean, *That Mexican* (Fleming H. Revell Company), p. 60.

But by the time the first priest reached my family party he had grown tired and careless. Instead of collecting the certificates singly, he began to take them in twos and threes with the result that they became mixed, and Geronimo was confirmed, not as Geronimo, but as "Saturnina," which happened to be the name of the little snubnosed Totonac girl standing next to him. When I realized what had happened, I protested. Whereupon his grace and I proceeded to have "words." With exceeding bitterness he then reperformed the rite, and if the eyes of the first priest could have killed, I should have withered on my slender stalk.[21]

Or consider a typical church scene in pre-Revolutionary Mexico.

A stout and venerable padre comes down the aisle, followed by a procession of choir boys in red and white. More than once he stops on his way to the little door in the choir to speak to one or another, and the women reverently kiss his fat hand. His kindly face seems to express approval of his generous proportions, as much as to say, "Let them fast and pray who will, but no fasting for me. . . . ." In the faces of the kneeling worshippers one sees the whole gamut of human expression. Such great wistful eyes look out from closely drawn rebosos; and now and again those so bold. Here are the suppliant and the penitent; criminal faces also, and those from which all human interest and feeling have faded and which look beyond to some shadowy hope not of this world. A swarthy little man, with bristling hair and moustache, prays long and fervently while his small pig-eyes rove this way and that, ceaselessly darting sly and furtive glances at those around. Near him a crippled woman has dragged herself to the railing on her knees by the aid of a pair of short crutches. Dropping the papers and lottery tickets she carried for sale, and grasping the iron bars, she burst into tears. Presently a fat old lady bustles up with much ado, crosses herself with an air, as if powdering her face, and bustles away again without so much as a glance at the others.[22]

[21] C. M. Flandrau, op. cit., pp. 55 f.

[22] Stanton Davis Kirkham, Mexican Trails (G. P. Putnam's Sons, 1909), p. 18.

Church ritual in Mexico has always been largely a matter of the letter rather than the spirit. Anyone who has visited a Church cemetery has seen the large pile of bones which have been cast out of the crypts and dug out of the graves as soon as the rental was unpaid, for the rentals in consecrated ground must be paid *in perpetuum.* Since the government has taken over all cemeteries, this practice has been discontinued.

The Church's lack of moral guidance did not stop here, it is charged. Persons failing to get the Church's blessing on their unions or on children born of these lawless unions could still get full blessings on the deferred-payment plan. Any time that the contracting parties found the necessary money for the fee they came to the priest and received the same consecration they would have received had they lived in solitary virtue until they could afford a lawful marriage. The priest did not then tell these violators of the moral code that they had sinned but would be forgiven. He did not say, "Go and sin no more." He merely took the fee and said nothing.

Last year a man I know, who has a cattle ranch a day and a half away from here, issued a general invitation to the countryside to come to his place and be married free of charge. He built a temporary chapel and hired a priest and for two days the hymeneal torch flamed as it never had in that part of the world before. So many persons took advantage of the opportunity that the priest, who began by marrying a couple at a time, was obliged toward the last to line them up in little squads of six and eight and ten and let them have it, so to speak, by the wholesale. It was pathetic to see old men and women with their children and their children's children all waiting in the same group to be married.[23]

Another eyewitness, twenty years later, tells the same story in an entirely different part of the Republic. On August 1,

[23] C. M. Flandrau, *Viva Mexico,* p. 127.

1926, the Mexican clergy started a Church strike that lasted for three years in an effort to thwart the government in its attempt to carry out the provisions of the national constitution. During the last week before the calling of the strike the Cathedral in Mexico City was crowded with persons seeking indulgences for their past shortcomings. Activity during one day is thus described:

The Indians—the poor and the disinherited—were the ones fighting for this last-minute salvation. The middle and upper classes were not forced to this extremity. Their children had been baptized, christened, confirmed, married at leisure. But the masses streaming into the church had to postpone these liturgical acts from week to week, hoping against hope that next month or the month after a few pennies could be laid aside for the confirmation veil, the necessary candles, the fees. But now in this last minute scramble they cheated their stomachs and mortgaged their health to beg, borrow, or steal the sums required for every holy act, every administration of holy water, every declaration of bans. . . . . this vast pawing scramble of the excited disinherited of Mexico, this flaunting of idolatry, superstition, rags, dirt, was a profanation of the human spirit. The Mexican-Spanish-Aztec church in its battle with the Mexican state showed a callous cruelty, reminiscent of the days of Innocent III.[24]

Evidence could be accumulated indefinitely to support the stand of the present-day Mexican government in its fight against superstition, fanaticism, and immorality. This résumé is intended to give the government's justification for its stand in regard to secularization of the schools. As the Church has resisted to the utmost the right of the government to handle education, the government has had to fight back. It has fought back by requiring that all priests shall be Mexicans, that they shall not have the right to

[24] Carleton Beals, *Mexican Maze* (J. B. Lippincott Company), pp. 287–89.

vote or to appear in public in their clerical habiliments. Some of the states have gone further and allow only priests who are married to officiate. The place of the schools is that of an active agent in freeing the minds of a new generation from the slavery of the past.

THE PLACE OF SCIENCE AND RATIONALISM IN MEXICO'S SCHOOLS

How, then, does the Socialist school intend to give the people freedom of mind and conscience while it is supporting the government's struggle against the Church? Does it intend to make a religion of science? School leaders answer that they are not attacking religion and that they do not intend science to supplant religion; they merely wish the people to get a modern view of the universe and enjoy any religion they choose. In short, they are attempting to reach the same position that the United States today occupies in her educational fields.

. . . . The restrictions placed by Mexico on the nature of elementary education, however drastic they might be from the standpoint of religious instruction, are those to which the schools in the United States have conformed in principle. While Americans may regret that the Mexican Church has been deprived of this medium of religious education, there is no consistency in denying that the Mexican programme of federal schools is grounded on a sound principle of education in a democracy.[25]

In so far as the school participates in the struggle between Church and state, it is only in the field of breaking the hold of idolatry, superstition, and fear of supernatural angers.[26] It is further forced to battle for its own legal

[25] George I. Sanchez, *op. cit.*, p. 175.
[26] Ignacio Garcia Tellez, *Socialización de la Cultura*, pp. 37–38.

and constitutional existence, for the Church has fomented lawlessness, defiance of the Constitution, and bloodshed. Modern rationalism may not hold the key to all life's processes. But the Church in Mexico fears enlightenment, and wherever possible it still fights secular education. Recently in San Pablo Etla, I found that the priest was declaiming from the pulpit against the Federal school and incited some of the villagers to tear up the athletic field. In most rural localities the priest threatens parents with dire punishments if they permit their children to attend government schools. In a small village in the Mixtecan Indian region, the people were frightened by the wailing of La Llorana, the ghost of Maliche (bed-companion of Cortes) that prowled the streets every night. The military commandant of the region, on visiting the village, heard this nightly terror and set his soldiers to catch the spook. It proved to be the sacristan dressed up in a sheet and a frightful mask.[27]

It is exactly this appeal to the pagan fears of the people that the school is fighting. The school teacher declares that his appeal is to love and light and cleanliness as opposed to fear and darkness and ignorance. From time to time in the body of this study notice has been taken of the way in which the religious and so-called respectable people of Mexico have fought and thwarted the work of the school. They have fought it in its anti-alcoholic campaign, they have fought it in its attempts to bring the lessons of science to the people, and they have fought it in its attempts to teach the peasants better farming methods.

The school has taken over many of the techniques of spiritual catharsis and is using them in the curriculum. Thus music is enjoying a renaissance in Mexico through the efforts of the schools. Regional music has been gathered and is made available to schools throughout the country. Painting is in evidence everywhere, without the gloom

[27] Carleton Beals, *Mexican Maze* (J. B. Lippincott Company), p. 297.

and lewdness that once characterized Mexican art. Dancing is taught in the federal schools with a new air of cleanliness and decency that does not demand a sexual and drinking debauch afterward. The school people do not take the laissez faire attitude of the clergy toward license; when there is depravity, the school teacher and his pupils are somewhere else.

Fireworks, folk-plays with all delicacy left out, everybody in town who can get there, and unlimited supplies of liquor. It was a fiesta with no trace of today at all. The teachers had gone to the baseball game with the modern young Mexicans.[28]

A science is being offered the new Mexico that will mean a new way of life. It is not a mysterious science that is aimed at making life less meaningful, but one that will fill the world with meaning. Botany teaches the Mexican the true mysteries of the germinating and burgeoning *maiz*. Natural science teaches him why the life-giving rain comes and perhaps replaces primeval vestiges of a belief in and worship of Tlaloc but certainly does not replace belief in a Supreme Being who makes natural law. Chemistry teaches him why he should improve his diet and how he can increase the fecundity of his soil without offering sacrifices to regional gods or indulging in sympathetic magic to propitiate the goddess of fertility. It perhaps shows him the futility of paying a priest to bless the grain that is to be planted. Hygiene teaches the student that he should have sanitary drinking water so that he need no longer drink from the drain that runs down the middle of the street. Biology will teach the Mexican school boy and girl how the body functions, how to rid the body of germs, how to exercise properly, and why one should not drink alcoholic beverages.

[28] Erna Fergusson, *op. cit.*, p. 40.

In the course of this education and its application Mexico will lose many of her picturesque customs in another generation. Women will not wrap their heads tightly in *rebozos* to keep out the fresh air; they will not lay babies on the fly-covered floors of markets. Houses will be built more spaciously to give proper ventilation and more hygienic quarters for the family. Undoubtedly the infant-mortality rate will drop from a point perilously close to 50 per cent to one approaching that of the United States. Fear, both economic and supernatural, will disappear and the Mexican will be a happy individual who more closely resembles his Maker and is not "half-brother to the ox." It was the author's privilege to talk with Edwin Markham in the shadow of the pyramid at San Juan Teotihuacán. The venerable poet said then that the Mexican came nearer to his concept of "The Man with the Hoe" than any class or race he had encountered.

Indubitably much of the "color" of Mexico will be lost for bored tourists and visiting writers. But the contention of the Mexican educator is that it is better for Mexico to be the home of a healthy, happy, modern race than to be a curiosity for the rest of the world to pity and stare at for its picturesqueness. The sentimentalist regrets the passing of an anachronistic civilization and adds his weight to the force of the reactionaries who are fighting to keep their ancient right and privileges.

Future citizens were waiting on the cement platform ready to dance. A teacher in a heavy marcel and a bright red blouse marshaled them out to greet the visitors. This was the kindergarten, mites of four or five years, all very clean, and in the real indigenous costumes. Boys in white calzones, shirts, and sashes; girls in low blouses and pleated skirts. They ran and crowded, but not one forgot his manners. They spoke in gentle voices and offered soft warm baby hands at greeting and parting. Later they danced to a tune played on the piano, with fussy teachers bossing every move. It was well done, compared with the performance in the church—a tidy performance, well regulated, schooled, and trained. But where, oh where, was the indigenous dance? This came from the Secretaría de Educación in Mexico and had no connection with the ancient tribal rites of the place. They would have danced a Japanese dance with the same feeling.

At the other end of the school grounds, *besket-bol* was going on. It was an informal game with no uniforms, no coach, nothing that looked like supervision; but it was a hard, fast game, played according to rule, and it had attracted an audience of half a hundred men and boys, while the dances in the church and at the school were watched by only the doting parents.

Those two dances and the game represent something significant that is happening in Mexico, something that even a stranger feels poignantly, that probably not even the most thoughtful Mexican could fully analyze. Serious students find many approaches to the problem, but anyone who looks at fiestas must be aware of the complications made by the Church and school sport—everything that touches youth and influences it. What is going to happen to these children? Not the nation, but the people. For four hundred years they have lived in the way approved by the Roman Catholic Church. They have functioned within that scheme in ways of their own. Their saints are gods of their own little place. They honor Christian saints with pagan customs, but, for all that, life has centered in the Church. Now, suddenly, a government as remote to most of them as the north star has decided that they must no longer live that way. Taking the Church away, if it can be done, will mean taking away much that all humanity needs, especially simple humanity that cannot find reassurance in mental exercises. In spite of all that may be said of the abuses of the clergy, the Church offers comfort; see any Indian kneeling to his saint. It offers pageantry and drama: human drama, simple enough to enthrall the most childish mind, deeply human enough to have meaning for the most sophisticated. It offers beauty in statue and picture, music and candlelight, robes and vestments, churches as lovely as jewels, and veritable jewels worn by the loveliest Madonnas and handled by girls and women who could never have such things for themselves. It offers gayety and fun. And it offers a spiritual way of life.[29]

Such rationalizations, say the educators, do not explain the tremendous cost these baubles represent to the people.

There is perhaps no country equally civilized where the educational, political, and material welfare of the laboring people has advanced less and where their condition presents more cruel, and at the same time more immemorially picturesque phases than in Mexico. The problem of lifting them to a distinctly higher plane of life is the immediate and urgent problem of the nation. It was the justification for the Madero revolution, whatever may have been the alleged grievances of other classes. It is the matter concerning which the Díaz regime must give its most important final account, however great the progress made in material development.[30]

Certainly a new spirit is abroad in Mexico, compounded of the forces of morality, psychology, biology, chemistry, and learning in all its ramifications. Arrayed against this spirit are the forces of *mortemain,* entrenched privilege, and conservatism.

Another factor which the Church in Mexico—as elsewhere—must face is the general trend of modern philosophy, whose principles and ideas are incompatible with the platonic absolutism of the Catholic dogmas. Miracles have not yet reconciled themselves with modern science. All the anti-Catholic tendencies of modern thought have converged in the minds of the living Mexican intellectuals—Caso, Vasconcelos, Lombardo Toledano, Rivera, Reyes, Dr. Atl. Not only modern thinking but the modern system challenges the Church— all the tremendous material expansion of our day. It is with true instinct that the National League of Religious Defense in Mexico instituted an economic boycott against luxuries— autos, amusements, fine clothes, and epicurean foods—in its

[29] Erna Fergusson, *Fiesta in Mexico* (Alfred Knopf), pp. 251–52.

[30] E. H. Blichfeldt, *A Mexican Journey* (The Chautauqua Press, 1912), pp. 12–13.

war with the Government. (The saving went to pay for boot-
leg masses at fifty pesos a head.) The Church boycott failed,
not because its members had become leisure-loving (its priests
perhaps), but because the mass of people in Mexico are denied
even the minimum of life's necessities.[31]

Mexican intellectuals say their country is definitely making a change; she is trading one way of life for another
with her eyes open. Mexico is not repudiating Christ nor
his teachings; she is attempting to go back to his precepts
and put them into practice. Like most other revolts against
the Church, this revolt is against dead formalism rather
than the essence of religion.

On the threshold it may be noted that throughout all the
centuries of destructive criticism the character of Jesus Christ
has never been besmirched.[32]

Mexico's stand is best shown by a phrase used in a modern
Mexican school reader.[33] *No Cristo Rey, sino Cristo
Pueblo,* "not Christ the king but the people's Christ."

[31] Carleton Beals, *Mexican Maze* (J. B. Lippincott Company), pp.
296–97.

[32] E. L. Pennington, "The Revolt against Christianity," *The American Scholar,* Spring, 1937.

[33] E. V. Bringas, *Lecturas Populares,* p. 259.

Newspaper mural showing Nazism and Fascism.
executing the "Dance Macabre."

A newspaper mural in the national normal
school protesting Nazism and Fascism.

Chapter IV

REVOLUTIONARY ART IN SCHOOL AND SOCIETY

Because the school is so inextricably bound up in society, school art and the art of the nation are almost indistinguishable. Most Mexican artists are teachers and, conversely, most teachers of art are artists. Art life in Mexico centers in the Secretariat of Education with its colorful frescoes and paintings by subsidized artists. The Department of Education has been the constant patron of art since Vasconcelos built the new Secretariat and the National Normal School. To a race that transmits ideas pictorially, that is accustomed to architectonic masterpieces as a part of its everyday life, and that draws pictures on any blank wall where other races would scribble, the surest means of communicating new dogma is through the ramifications of art. For these reasons art has become one of the most potent tools of indoctrination in the new school of Mexico.

Since the close of the Revolution in 1921, two schools of art have existed side by side. The formal, or Beaux Arts, has of necessity been traditional and exotic, a European graft on the Mexican stalk. The newer, Revolutionary art, which is variously designated as proletarian and materialistic, has been an evolutionary concomitant of the social growth of the nation. Like Topsy, it "just growed" from the loves and hates and hopes and fears of the people.

In the Fine Arts Academy, students made dancing nymphs for bedrooms and recast Greek casts . . . . Outside the Academy Guadalupe Posada anonymously laughed and wept and created an art by himself, illustrating ballads. Other anonymous people painted miracles on tin or cardboard and hung them with prayers in their favourite shrines. Or murals in the city streets, on the walls of *pulquerías*.¹ . . . .

BIRTH OF MEXICAN POPULAR ART

Guadalupe Posada worked quite frankly for the man on the street. His work was to illustrate *corridos,* those wholly Mexican ballads that take the place of newspaper, show, or radio throughout the nation. Of the *corrido* Robert Redfield says:

> The essential difference between the *corrido* and the folk song of the truly primitive people appears to lie in the tendency of the *corrido* to enter into the realm of news, public opinion and even propaganda.²

Posada turned from the stylized European form to one that was realistic and Mexican. Up to his time peasants had been portrayed whenever they were treated, which was seldom, in an Arcadian and wholly artificial manner. The artist, like the rest of the ruling class, considered the native as being without significance as a subject or as an audience.³ Painting was as far removed from life as possible; scenes worthy of reproduction were taken from the Bible, history, or court life.

Posada broke sharply with all this. His woodcuts and zinc etchings changed, the latter in technique as well as in style. His work is ludicrous, caricature; yet it is essen-

¹ Anita Brenner, *Idols behind Altars,* pp. 98–99.

² *Tepoztlan: A Mexican Village* (The University of Chicago Press), p. 9.

³ Roberto Montenegro, *Mexican Painting, passim.*

tially tragic; it is Pagliacci in a line drawing. He did all his work during the régime of Díaz and the early days of the Revolution, dying when the thing he had long hinted at was becoming a reality. In the midst of the decay of the *ancien régime* he dared to depict the aristocracy as decadent and perverted, and to present riots, plagues, and virtual slavery when such things were officially ignored. Above all he caught Mexico on the point of the etching tool and transferred it to metal that is still producing copies. He gave the world the types that are still drawing cries of protest as they appear in the work of the increasing hordes of young revolutionary artists.

When José Vasconcelos became Secretary of Education in 1921 he attempted to formulate the chaotic surge of the Revolution into education. For Director of Drawing[4] he chose Adolfo Best-Maugard. Like Posada, Best-Maugard attempted to foment an art that was essentially Mexican and to do this he went back to the pre-Conquest Mexico of the Aztec and Maya.[5] Fifteen years before, while doing archaeological drawing for Professor Franz Boas, he had decided that seven fundamental motifs underlay the work of the ancients. By combining these basic designs, the most involved drawings could be developed. All of this artistic dialect, then, might be expected to lead to higher values. As Best-Maugard put it,

> The important part in the new conception will be the work, its aesthetic function. Being no longer circumstantial but transcendental, and of a higher category, the work of the artist will comprise conscious knowledge of its causes—its function and its purpose.[6]

[4] *Dirección de Dibujo.*

[5] Robert N. McLean, *That Mexican*, p. 96.

[6] Adolfo Best-Maugard, *A Method for Creative Design* (Alfred A. Knopf), p. 173.

This aesthetic vagueness, true of the entire post-Revolutionary group of educators and artists, was the cause of Vasconcelos' removal from office and his later reappearance in one of Rivera's murals—seated on a white elephant. Best-Maugard and his book were both removed, quite without animus, to serve as historical curiosities.

El libro donde Adolfo Best desarrolló los postulados de su teoría, si no adquiere importancia y valor educativos, no pierde su merito de curiosidad.[7]

The new Director of Drawing, Manuel Rodriguez Lozano, himself an artist of note, introduced the method based on self-expression. The pedagogy smacks strongly of John Dewey, whose teachings were seeping across the Rio Bravo, brought by former students, and through translations of his works. During the 1920's the Mexican curriculum gave almost full sway to the Master of Morningside Heights. Where the credit goes is beside the point; the fact remains that art education became a matter of the child's becoming thoroughly liberated. He was to draw what he felt like drawing, and was not to be directed, thwarted, or inhibited.

Open-air art schools, originated by Alfredo Ramos Martinez in Coyoacan, became popular; and the government founded centers in especially picturesque spots such as Xochimilco, Cuernavaca, Tlalpam, Guadalajara, and Taxco. Products of the art schools were expected not only to furnish an index to the progress of the student and the school but to give data for psychological research. Color was stressed continually. In Mexico the child is conscious of color from the day on which his eyes can distinguish the spectrum until his eyesight fails. The green of the plateau, varying from sage to the bluish-green of

[7] X. Villaurrutia, "La Pintura Mexicana Actual," *Nuestro Mexico*, Noviembre 1932.

the ever-present maguey, and the lush green of the tropics
are always given an appropriate background by the mountains. The mountains of Mexico are ubiquitous, and range
in color from the lightest lavender to a crude purple that
Maxfield Parrish would not dare to attempt. Behind these,
and providing constant points of accent, are the majestic
snow-covered volcanoes that have become an almost symbolic part of Mexican art.

RISE OF THE SCHOOL OF MONUMENTAL ART

Concomitant with the development of popular education
in art was the rise of the fresco painters. Diego Rivera
returned from a ten-year stay in Europe, where he studied
in Spain, Belgium, Holland, France, and Italy. In France,
Rivera came under the influence of Cezanne and Renoir,
generally accepted as the founders of the school of monumental art. This inspiration caused him to finish his study
in Italy in the field of Italian fresco. He returned to Mexico to find it aflame with Revolutionary ideology and a
resurgence of interest in indigenous Mexico, particularly
the Indian.[8] Rivera toured southern Mexico and Yucatan,
filling his sketchbooks with types and typical scenes. He
also discovered that fresco had been raised to a high degree by the Mayas of the new empire, whose technique
was distinguished and whose formula for a mural paint
was unexcelled.[9] Many of the edifices discovered by ar-
chaeologists contained murals that remained almost un-
dimmed in freshness after having been abandoned hundreds of years.

[8] Robert N. McLean, *That Mexican*, p. 95.
[9] T. A. Joyce, *Maya and Mexican Art*, p. 129; Alma Reed (editor),
José Clemente Orozco, p. 3; J. Eric Thompson, *The Civilization of the
Mayas*, pp. 87–88; J. Leslie Mitchell, *Conquest of the Maya*, pp. 89–90;
Laurence E. Schmeckebier, *Modern Mexican Art*, chapter i.

Rivera gathered about himself a talented group of painters imbued with the Revolutionary dogma. This group formed the Revolutionary Syndicate of Technical Workers, Painters, and Sculptors. They became a professional proletariat, vying with each other to be more like the workman than the laborer. They decreed:

Art for art's sake is an aesthetic fallacy; art for the people is a phrase of inconsistent and hypocritical sentimentalism. Art is necessarily a thing of the people, not an abstract concept, nor a vehicle for exploiting whims. The search for true expression of mass feeling is not to be confused with the doctrine that plastic art, to be reconstructive or revolutionary, must be subservient to the propagation of prescribed ideas. A panel sincerely and forcefully conceived from pure emotion, and portrayed according to the aesthetic laws of the craft, will generate its own *morale*.[10]

The chief actors in this artistic drama were: José Clemente Orozco, Alfaro Siqueiros, Carlos Mérida, Fermín Revueltas, Roberto Montenegro, Fernando Leal, Xavier Guerrero, Amado de la Cueva, and the Frenchman, Jean Charlot.

The group was given the National Preparatory School to paint. The Secretary of Education paid them on the same basis as house painters. During the two years the group worked in the cloisters, halls, and patios of the National Preparatory School was born the soul that now animates Mexican art, education, and architecture. The temperamental individualism that one thinks of in connection with the artist was sloughed off and there developed a true collective art. One must keep constantly in mind their manifesto, in order to follow the consistency of their art which many critics and visitors find chaotic. Their art is not for art's sake nor for the people's sake; it is of the

[10] Quoted by Anita Brenner, *Idols behind Altars* (Harcourt, Brace & Co.), p. 245.

people. They do not attempt to paint dogma unless they are at the time full of a dogma that burns to be given artistic or plastic birth. When they paint men and women they are not presenting sordid or distorted types that fuse into misanthropic impressionism. No; they are presenting Indians and *mestizos* as they are, broken, depraved beings showing the results of exploitation; or they portray dignified Tehuantepecs and clean-limbed Indians lacking the defects of an artificial civilization. The one concept directs attention to false standards; the other is expected to bring a new unity and dignity to the indigenous Mexican.

The Syndicate was composed almost equally of social reformers and Revolutionaries who were painters, and painters who were interested in Revolutionary ideas and social reform. Two years of intimate collaboration fused their thinking and execution into such an organic whole that they thought and painted as a unit. It is said that Siqueiros left work early one night to meet an engagement, leaving a partially completed panel. His coadjutor Guerrero obligingly put a head in. The execution pleased Siqueiros so mightily that he said it must be a miracle, and so provided for another with a head that was more Siqueiros than one by Siqueiros himself.

After their long working day the group went into other fields with unquenched fire. They edited and filled the *Machete* with articles, editorials, and woodcuts. They lectured, attended union meetings, argued, made love, drank, and in general lived with gusto. Their painting was not a thing apart; it was definitely a thing they lived and believed in. Many of the group had fought in the Revolution or had come from the exploited masses they pictorialized. Their interest in the proletariat was not academic; it was functional.

As their work progressed, storms of protest raged about

them. They went to work unperturbed but with loaded pistols peeking from their overalls pocket. A group of ladies held a social function in the inner court of the Preparatoria and, to spare the delicate feelings of the guest, covered Orozco's monumental figures with drapes and boughs. A few weeks later a finished panel stood forth showing leaders tramping over the recumbent figures of the poverty-stricken and exploited classes. The ladies in it had their eyes and noses chastely averted so they would not be offended by sights and odors.

Soon vandals were at work; panels were mutilated, scratched, and stoned. A panel by Siqueiros remains unfinished to this day. With the end of the Obregón régime came the conclusion of the work at the Preparatoria and the demise of the Syndicate. Oddly enough, only two artists were retained by the government for continued work at the Secretariat of Education—Roberto Montenegro and Diego Rivera. Montenegro is famous for his style, while Rivera undoubtedly gave evidence of the opportunism of which he is accused by his contemporaries today. Certainly his work on the Preparatory School can hardly be called the most distinguished.

The members of the Syndicate scattered to different parts of the Republic. De la Cueva and Siqueiros went to Guadalajara, where they painted walls in the University, the state capitol, and the governor's mansion. A few days after the completion of their work De la Cueva was killed in an accident. Siqueiros turned from painting to labor and peasant organization and built up a powerful group. Later he visited the United States, where his activities caused his deportation. More social work in Mexico followed. When the war in Spain started he became tremendously stirred; for he knew Spain, both politically and artistically, from study there. Soon he followed his sympathies to Spain and, joining its government forces, offered his life for the ideals he had painted so ardently. Siqueiros is the archetype of the spirit of the Syndicate and of Mexican proletarian art today. It is an art that is so alive, so believed in by the artist, that it seems brutal to the patron who is accustomed to the salon art of the domesticated artist. Out of the Syndicate a spirit was synthesized that today animates the work of some one hundred artists and thousands of students in all the schools of Mexico. A few principles and symbols underlie the entire movement and serve as keys to unlock the door to understanding of any picture, wood carving, or mural executed by the modern school.

IDEOLOGICAL BASES OF REVOLUTIONARY ART

The poetry of Shelley has been called Godwin's *Political Justice* set to meter; similarly, the painting of the proletarian artists of Mexico may be called Karl Marx pictorialized. Their art is international, yet it is supremely American; that is to say, it is Mexican. The ideology, the symbols, the techniques have been found that are part of the country and yet they curiously fit into the Marxian cosmos. The Mexican has his centuries-old proverb from Netzahualcoyotl, Aztec poet-king: "The land belongs to him who works it with his hands." The spontaneous uprisings in Mexico from the time of the Conquest all were over practically the same thing—land. Zapata was the apotheosis of the national urge for "Land and Liberty." Thus thousands who perhaps never heard the name of Marx or Engels gave impetus to the urge to take land forcibly from those who held more than their share. This land consciousness explains the perennial peasant that one finds in so much of the new Mexican painting, both adult and student. The *campesino* stands with his sickle in convenient juxtaposition to the hammer of his friend, the workman, thus forming a fortuitous Communist symbol.

Another convention frequently encountered is the armed farmer. Through the four centuries of oppression the Indian learned to move off his land when ordered to do so. Land was taken unjustly and illegally; yet the Indian and the *mestizo* had no recourse but to get off. If they attempted resistance they were excommunicated and branded as outlaws and their punishment in the long run was far more severe than the mere losing of their land. The labor and agrarian leaders of today are now attempting to arouse in the *campesino* a spirit of resistance, the will to fight for what he believes to be rightly his, and to keep it once he has it. All of the force of the Marxian world is expected to come from the worker, the farmer, and the soldier. These three are pictured together so often that they have become almost a holy trinity. In one of Rivera's murals in the Secretariat of Education the three are pictured sneering at the white-collar workers and the bourgeois intelligentsia, and the legend over the panel reads: "All the real things in the world come from the soil."

Another urge that is spontaneously Mexican and at the same time a prime Marxian tenet is the desire for education. All over the nation the people are pleading and clamoring for land and schools. They will build the schools themselves if the government will only find teachers and keep them going. The keystone of the Socialist Mexican structure is, *Educar es redemir:* "To educate is to redeem." Again and again one finds a series of murals or pictures showing the coming of the new world with the historical approach. First come the exploiters: Spanish soldier, *hacendado*, and priest. Next the years of disgrace and oppression are shown; then comes the struggle, with the leader or perhaps an unknown soldier of the people killed. Later is shown the Revolution triumphant, with the new day dawning. In the last space or panel is almost always the school or schoolteacher, as the promise that all is well and the world well saved. These materials form the constant theme of Rivera and his satellites in any medium. In the auditorium of the Casa del Pueblo at Hermosillo, Sonora, is a sectioned stained-glass window designed by Revueltas and executed by Casa Montaña; the six scenes build up to the last one, which shows the Socialist schoolteacher instructing two children. Either intentionally or unconsciously the background of foliage gives the appearance of angel's wings. Time and again a tinge of Christian symbolism creeps into the new art; whether it is a device used to satisfy the conditioned desire of the Christianized masses or is fortuitous has not been satisfactorily answered. The use of the trinity of soldier, *campesino,* and worker by Rivera is almost ritualitsic.

THE INFLUENCE OF DIEGO RIVERA

Undoubtedly the Titan of the Revolutionary art movement in Mexico is Diego Rivera. The impress of his personality and work will be felt for years, possibly for centuries. He has already stimulated bitter controversies throughout the world. While a guest of the Soviet government in Moscow, he precipitated a rift in the artistic world there over Proletarian art. In the United States he caused a prolonged controversy with his murals, later removed, in the Rockefeller Center building. In his own country he has been an artistic stormy petrel since his return from Europe in 1921.

Not only the painters, but the teachers, the poets, the actors, the musicians, the students, and above all the foreigners, succumb to his rhythmic and massive insistence.[11]

[11] Anita Brenner, *Idols behind Altars,* pp. 286–87.

He is even given credit for revolt in the field of architecture.

This revolt, surprisingly enough, came not from the architects but from a group of painters, led by Diego Rivera.[12]

To understand why Rivera antagonizes conventional artists, Church leaders, society folk, and rich property holders it is necessary to analyze his artistic intentions. In general his philosophy is consonant with that of the government and school leaders so that the person who understands that ideology only has to learn Rivera's symbolism in order to understand the lessons inherent in his murals. Rivera himself has been quoted as saying of his aim:

If my work has a purpose, it may be summed up as being to make the greatest contribution of which I am capable to the esthetic nourishment of the working class, in the form of clarifying expression of the things that class must understand in its struggle for a classless society.[18]

Artists immediately reply that this is a negation of art, a commercialization, a prostitution of the muse. Art, they postulate, must be free; it must point no moral, take no sides in the mundane affairs of the world; it must be "Art for art's sake." At this point Rivera points to the materialist concept of art as formulated by Marx, Engels, Lunacharsky, Bukharin, and others. According to this group, art has always reflected the economic wants and desires of the ruling classes:

El arte es una manifestación de la conciencia, de la ideología y de la práctica social.[14]

Therefore the artist is, in reality, taking sides in the

---

[12] Beach Riley, "Social Progress and the New Architecture," *Architectural Record*, April 1937.

[18] Diego Rivera, *Portrait of America* (Covici-Friede), pp. 19–20.

[14] Arqueles Vela, *Historia Materialista de Arte*, p. 5.

struggle of the classes. He is either rich enough to live a life of leisure through individual wealth, or his clientele comes from the ruling class. His art contributes to the status quo in one way or another. They point out the way in which art glorifies the dominant institutions. Thus the artist, in the Middle Ages, produced vast amounts of ecclesiastical art which was in support of the Church and the feudal system. Bourgeois art has always been working for the interests of the ruling classes, they say, and has consistently ignored both the interests of the working classes and the material to be found in their *milieu*. Let the new Proletarian art be as strong for the working class, but let it be perfectly honest with its votaries and with the world at large and announce its purpose, say Rivera and his school.

Having postulated the apologia of Materialistic art, Rivera turns to fundamental techniques based on psychology, Indian Mexico, and Marxian ideology. As the goal of the Marxian is collectivism, so the aim of his painting is collective:

> The social development of our time is a continuous, accelerated march towards collectivization, and for this reason the necessity for mural painting, the character of which is essentially collective, becomes ever more urgent.[15]

His art is a portrayal of the masses for the masses. One thinks of masses every time he sees a panel or a complete mural. A criticism that one hears constantly in regard to Diego's work is that he does not paint beauty. Such a criticism is relative. Beauty is an abstract standard that resides in the beholder's mind. It is a factor conditioned by social training and usage. To the agrarian a large, fecund woman is beautiful because she is capable of bear-

---

[15] Diego Rivera, *op. cit.*, p. 11.

ing many children and doing much work on the farm. To the Chinese aristocrat long fingernails and obesity are beautiful because they show that he does not have to work. So the standard of beauty is a shifting norm that is set by society and by economic factors.

For this reason Rivera is attempting to set new standards of beauty. One must remember his esthetic bases are anti-imperialism, communism, and a glorification of the Indian. To achieve these effects he presents the Indian man or woman with stolid face and body, brown skin and strong square hands as a model of beauty. When he shows the white, it is with weak, effeminate face and body, and with long, soft, tapering hands. Work is the touchstone of beauty; whatever is useful, functional, is beautiful, whether it be a team of oxen, a woman with a water jar on her head, a modern machine, or a sky-scraper. This helps to explain the reason why he presents the indigenous type of Mexican working with the latest-type tractor. He is not interested in the picturesque; he rarely shows a scene in which the peon is working under primitive conditions. Like the philosophy of the government, that of Rivera is to encourage the salvaging of the good things handed down from the Toltec and Mayan civilizations but to jettison outmoded equipment. Rivera shocks the sentimentalist by lumping wooden plows, un-potable water, the Catholic Church, the class system, prostitution, ignorance, and bad roads in the same category.

While Rivera rarely has conventional beauty in individual faces, he achieves beauty in the ensemble. He is painting masses and to him the mass is the point of accent. The only individual who is beautiful is the worker or soldier dead for the cause or the Revolutionary leader killed by the forces of reaction. In all of his murals some one leader is accented. Thus one finds such figures as Zapata, Cabrillo, murdered governor of Yucatan, or Morelos high-lighted. Nearly all of his murals show the burial of a worker with the almost ritualistic mourning comrades. The murals of Rivera are monumental. They must be seen in their entirety to convey the cosmic surge that is immanent in them. They are a symphony of movement, ideas, myths, forces, but above all of people:

"Diego Rivera encierra en sus frescos todo el tumulto de mitos y de maquinas en un ritmo de grandes y amplios contrastes liricos."[16]

Truly there is a "tumult of myth and machine." Rivera would replace the Mexico of folklore and superstition with a Mexico of science and logic. Logic is the underlying stratum of his life, and he is forever transferring it to plaster. To him the smoothly functioning machine is the artifact of the greatest beauty in the world. It was conceived and built in harmony, conforming to the laws of mechanics, in conflict with no natural laws. To him it seems obvious that human life, human society can be organized on as rationalistic a basis.

He is fascinated by the machine and loves to paint it in motion. He sees in it a marvelous creation of the productive labor of mankind, a powerful and obedient servant of the producers in the mastery of nature, a thing of great esthetic beauty in its firmness and precision, in the might and subtlety of its motion, in the clarity of its lines, and the unerring expression of function in its structure.[17]

THE MURALS OF RIVERA

Rivera has important murals in both the United States and Mexico. His North American frescoes are found

---

[16] Arqueles Vela, *op. cit.*, p. 78.
[17] Bertram Wolfe, in *Portrait of America* (Covici-Friede), p. 163.

in San Francisco in the Stock Exchange and the School of Fine Arts; in the Detroit Museum; and in New York in the New Workers' School. In Mexico important murals are located in the National Preparatory School, the National Palace, the Palace of Fine Arts, and the Secretariat of Public Education in Mexico City; in the Agricultural School at Chapingo; and in Cortes' Palace in Cuernavaca. The murals at Chapingo are perhaps the most distinguished and unified of his works. They are painted on the walls and ceilings of a small assembly hall that was formerly a chapel. The work is finished in technique and highly symbolic. All the symbolism is purposely different from the conventional. It is reminiscent of Shelley's "Revolt of Islam," in which Shelley had a serpent represent the force of good and an eagle that of evil. The dominant figure of the room is a semi-reclining nude woman on the back wall. She represents Mother Nature. Below her Father Nature is giving fire to man. This scene immediately brings to mind the beautiful story of Prometheus; but one must be warned vigorously that this figure is not that of Prometheus, for he stole the fire to give to man. According to the Rivera cosmogony, fire is man's right and it is given him freely by Father Nature.

The work in the National Palace consists of one tremendous picture representing the pageant of Mexico. It is meaningless to the person unacquainted with Mexican history, for each figure represents a historical figure or a symbolic personage. It is a symphony of history in color. Rivera's famous mural in the Palace of Fine Arts is a replica of the destroyed central panel in the Rockefeller Center. In the auditorium of the National Preparatory School is to be found a Rivera that is interesting only as a forerunner of what the *maestro* was to do later.

Who would eat must work, says this mural of Rivera's.

The Mexican teacher is shown helping all classes of society in this Rivera mural.

There is enough for all classes in Mexico, suggests this mural by Rivera.

The murals in the Palace of Cortes at Cuernavaca were paid for by Dwight Morrow, former United States Ambassador to Mexico, and are his gift to the people of Cuernavaca. They are painted on the exterior stucco of an outside corridor overlooking the plains of Morelos. In the distance Popocatepetl sleeps in ageless majesty. This mural took ten months to paint and is remarkable for the dominant green of certain of the panels, a green that is the color of the cane fields of Morelos. The panel which shows the Indians bringing the first fruits to the priests is considered most typical of the light in which the Revolutionaries place the Church. Monks and priests are depicted with cruel, rapacious faces and well-fed figures clothed in ample, well-made garments. They are accepting baskets of fruit, bread, meat, and food from the half-naked barefoot natives. One Indian reaches over the carcass of a newly killed deer to kiss the hem of a monk's robe. A woman, kneeling, offers a basket of fruit; two other Indians are in positions of humility, one kissing a monk's hand, another offering a basket of precious stones. The hands of one monk are curved in cupidity as he reaches for the gift.

Most significant socially, if not artistically, of all Rivera's work are the frescoes in the Secretaría de Educación Publica. The murals are painted in the corridors that open on a tremendous interior court and extend for three stories upward. Even the prolific Rivera needed four years to finish this *magnum opus,* which is perhaps one of the major esthetic feats in the Americas.

He [Rivera] is probably the greatest painter of our time; and the Mexican epic which he has painted in the heart of its educational building may yet be esteemed as the greatest achievement in painting in the western hemisphere.[18]

[18] Ernest Gruening, *op. cit.,* p. 640.

On the first floor is found *México típico:* religious festivals, tropical Vera Cruz, the Yaqui Deer Dance, women of Tehuantepec, workers in the steel mills of Monterrey. Each panel is realistic; there is none of the nostalgic emotion of the escapist showing a heroic past or a Rousseauistic savage. There is seldom emotion in the work of Rivera; emotion is the forte of Orozco. In the feast of the Day of the Dead Rivera shows the festival as it is celebrated. There is all the tinsel and trapping of the Mexican fiesta: death's head masks, *campesinos* in sombreros, cheap, overdressed women, horn-blowers, puppet skeletons, and busy concessionaires selling *refrescos* and *antojitos*. The artist has even shown himself moving through the crowd in evident enjoyment of the noise and confusion.

On the first floor the artistic approach is geographical and historical. Interspersed with scenes showing dyers, harvesters, weavers, miners, smelters, and pottery makers are evolutionary panels presenting the birth and growth of the Revolution. A miner in Guanajuato is shown emerging from the mine to experience the daily humiliation of a search by the overseers. Next comes the death of a laborer in the early uprisings against oppression. Following this is the taking of the land with the orderly division of the *haciendas* by agronomists. Rivera not only shows the peasant what to do in his murals; he shows him how to do it. Thus in the division of the land, trained men—engineers, agronomists, and social leaders—supervise an orderly, equitable meeting at which the lands taken from the exploiters are inexorably divided among those who are to farm the fields. This theme is given a slightly different redaction in the stair well at Chapingo, where Diego has pictorialized the motto of the Agricultural School: "Exploit the earth, but not your fellow man."

Another significant section of the first floor finds three panels given over to the workers celebrating the First of May, that international holiday started by Chicago's Haymarket Riots. Over a door is a scroll with one of the ever present Rivera slogans; this one says, "True civilization will be achieved by a harmony of man with the earth and between men upon the earth." These panels are in perfect keeping with the rest of Rivera's work: there is little emotional presentation. Workers of all races are gathered in one vast concourse. A few have bandages, representing wounds received from the Cossacks. Zapata and Carrillo face each other; each lays a hand reassuringly upon the shoulders of a small boy.

On the third gallery are the burning, acerbic, doctrinaire panels which cause the protests from bourgeois beholders. Around the entire corridor run a series of individual panels connected ideologically rather than in a narrative fashion. The panels are connected by a riband of orange on which are refrains from ballads and *corridos*. The work is as colorful as an Indian painted for a war dance. These panels represent the epitome of artistic ridicule; here is undoubtedly the Mecca of Proletarian art— "cartoon elevated into art, and art become a weapon."[19]

These panels are on the way to becoming classics. They have been photographed and reproduced for sale in tourist literature and reprinted in magazines until certain ones are becoming legendary. There is the "Song of Zapata" in which the leader and his followers are singing to the strains of a guitar in the hands of a roly-poly *campesino*. The "Capitalist Family" shows an overdressed group about a table. All are prepared to start the banquet, and wait with forks poised. They are baffled, however,

[19] Ernestine Evans, *The Frescoes of Diego Rivera*, p. 14.

for there is nothing to eat but one solitary gold coin on each plate.

One picture expresses Rivera's theories of art perfectly. A strong, brown woman is cleaning house. She has rifle and cartridge belt, and is backed by armed worker, farmer, and soldier. Two overdressed aristocrats are standing helplessly by with looks of futility, while the brown woman points at the motto, which says: "Those that would eat must work." An artist in traditional smock and scarf is being kicked to the floor by a youth with rifle and emblem of the Syndicate. In this position the artist will have to eat his paintbrush, palette, and lyre. Another panel shows a young lady schoolteacher passing out books and materials of instruction to children, to adults, and to the triumvirate of soldier, farmer, and worker.

Whatever one thinks of the work of Rivera, he must admit that the man has influenced and will continue to influence thought and artistic theory for many years. His murals are in strategic places where hundreds of persons come in contact with them daily. In the Secretaría the life blood of the national school system pulses daily. Department heads, subsecretaries, supervisors, *misioneros,* teachers, and students hurry about their work continually. On each trip they receive a sensuous message that can never be forgotten.

THE CONTRIBUTION OF JOSÉ CLEMENTE OROZCO

While Rivera is the painter of the logical process of arriving at the collectivized world, Orozco is the apostle of emotion. Rivera builds up a series of static scenes, each of which is like a detail in a blueprint. Everything is ordered and in place; there is balance, and closed symmetry. Orozco presents an unbalanced world that is full of sham, injustice, hypocrisy, and stupidity. He is bitter, violently so; he is Mexico's Dean Swift.

Rivera es más dialéctico, y su forma está más cerca del conocimiento; Orozco es violento y mistico; mientras Rivera observa la vida y la refleja, racionalmente, Orozco trasluce una intensidad apasionada.[20]

Orozco, like Siqueiros and others of the Revolutionary artists, lived through the Revolution with the Red Brigade. His missing left hand kept him from active fighting, but he produced cartoons and text for an army publication and saw the war at first hand. One cannot help feeling that Rivera is a dodger of reality. He left Mexico just as the Revolution opened and remained in Europe until the very year in which the war ended. While in France his heart bled for the cause of the Allies, but some vague cause kept him from fighting for them. He espoused Proletarian art as he had impressionism, pointilism, futurism, and cubism. He must be given credit for thoroughness; once he had espoused a cause he became thoroughly grounded in its principles, but deep under it all the soul of Orozco is missing.

Orozco has pitifully little to show for his years of work and suffering. He is not the witty center of cosmopolitan groups that Rivera is. When he visited the United States, he did not find himself the vortex of titanic storms; he only suffered petty humiliation and mild curiosity. At the international border he was stopped by the artistic cognoscenti of the United States government, and one hundred of his drawings were burned. In Los Angeles he existed by tinting photographs. He executed one mural at Pomona College, Claremont, California, which has not attracted wide attention. Where Rivera is the pièce de résistance at any banquet, Orozco is the skeleton at the

[20] Arqueles Vela, *op. cit.*, p. 78.

feast. His burning eyes look out upon a world of traducers through unromantic, thick lenses.

Today he is reaping something of a reward in the attitude of the artistic leaders in Mexico. Everywhere he is considered one of them, a real Revolutionary, whereas Rivera is considered a charlatan, a seeker after kudos, an artist for the American *turistas*.

It is indubitable that Orozco's work in the Preparatoria was by far the most distinguished and at the same time the most vilified of the Syndicate.[21] That of Rivera in the same building is almost emasculate by comparison. Yet on its completion Rivera was kept on the government payroll and alowed to get four years' additional experience in the field of monumental art, while Orozco had to fend for himself in a decidedly hostile world. He did manage to pick up a meager livelihood as a newspaper caricaturist; but he lost the valuable years of experience working on the walls of important buildings. Rivera has been subsidized by individuals or groups all his life, while Orozco has been Ishmael, with every man's hand against him. In spite of these handicaps he has work small in quantity but so powerful in execution that the pendulum of discriminating taste is slowly swinging his way.

Orozco has a wall in the Casa de Azulejos, the "House of Tiles," or, to the tourist horde, simply Sanborn's. This task was definitely a commercial commission, paid for by Francisco Iturbe; yet Jean Charlot described it as the most beautiful wall painted in America. He has another mural in an industrial school in the city of Orizaba.

In the Palacio de Bellas Artes, Orozco has produced what is perhaps one of the most smashing Revolutionary murals in the world. The Renaissance word *terribilité* is the perfect name for the composition. The world of

[21] Alma Reed (editor), *José Clemente Orozco*, "Introduction."

capitalism, symbolized by intricate machinery with its slaves chained to it, is being overturned by the push of the new freed man. In the foreground is a full length, naked strumpet, Orozco's symbol of the immorality of capitalism. She too is about to be crushed by the relentless advance of the orderly ranks of the awakened proletariat. This fresco is on the third floor, at the opposite end of a great salon from Rivera's copy of the Rockefeller mural.

Orozco's art and irony reach a high point in his work at the Preparatoria, however. He has one scene—*La Trinchera*, "The Trench"—in which he has combined explosive dynamics with technical perfection. Three soldiers behind a stone bulwark are attempting to hold back some enormous thrust from the other side of the barrier. One soldier is down; another, evidently wounded, is giving the last of his strength in one tremendous heave; the remaining soldier faces toward the enemy and attempts to hold the crumbling barrier with the last of his will power. It is a perfect portrayal of the spirit of *No pasarán*, or *Ils ne passeront pas*. The influence of the artist's years as a caricaturist is everywhere apparent. His depiction of Liberty is a classic. She is a drunken bawd selling out to the wealthy, who are giving her a bacchanalian party. Justice negligently holds her tilted scales and leers at the world as she is embraced sensually by a *politico*. The entire work is a bitter indictment of a world run without social planning, sincerity, or scruple. "In the *Preparatoria* he seemed to have painted with a thousand horse power piston dipped in vitriol."[22]

Orozco's newest and most highly acclaimed work from the standpoint of Revolutionary art is found in his wall and cupola murals in the assembly hall at the University of Guadalajara. These frescoes serve as a measure of the

[22] Anita Brenner, *op. cit.*, p. 254.

growth of Materialistic art in Mexico and of the personal growth in technique and ideology of the artist in sixteen years. As Aragon says:

For if it is true that since his earliest work he has given utterance to that which has remained in Mexico unuttered throughout centuries, it is equally true that the murals at the Preparatory School lack the enormous wealth and intricacy evinced in his Guadalajara achievement.[23]

The painted dome is more than fifty feet in diameter, and its vast space has been worked into a unity that expresses both the simplicity and the complexity of Socialist thought.

The entire mural revolves about man. Man is the measure of the universe; he is the beginning and the end, the master and the slave. Man is answerable only to himself. Gone are gods, fables, allegories, and the Elysian fields of otherworldliness. There are four fundamental figures. One is man measuring and comparing his world. With square and compass he attempts to limit and understand his world. In front of him is a macabre figure, a cadaver ready to be dissected. This symbolizes man serving mankind. The third figure is the scientist, the man who makes use of the information gathered in the first two fields of mensurable science. Figure number four is an enormous man who grasps folds of red cloth, while about him swirl blood and fire. He symbolizes and exalts the tragedy of humanity: rebellion.

The walls continue and amplify the theme of man struggling, trying to understand himself, betraying himself. One vast panel shows the educational struggle graphically. It is called "False Teaching and the Human Problem." Bearded savants are shown at their books, pointing out specious doctrines, which they force people to believe in

[23] Luis Cardoza y Aragon, "New Murals by José Clemente Orozco," *Mexican Life,* December 1937.

Revolutionary art in Hermosillo. The social revolution, the death of the worker, and the revolutionary hand passing on the torch. Aztec sun in background.

Stained-glass detail. Socialist schoolteacher and students.

spite of the fact that the savants know their teachings to be false. One pedagogue has a knife in his hand, symbolic of the force used to make people believe socially accepted fable in the older era. The Socialist teacher is leading a group of ghoul-like figures, symbols of oppressed and exploited humanity, against traditional education. This fresco has the depth and sweep of a canto from Dante's *Inferno*. Revolutionary artists consider the work at Guadalajara as the apogee of fresco art in the new world. "Guadalajara is the mistress of the most beautiful frescoes in America," says one critic.[24]

Other artists there are in Mexico; in fact the list is increasing daily. However, it would be pointless to name them categorically. The L.E.A.R.—*Liga de Escrituras y Artistas Revolucionarias*—has almost one hundred artists on its rolls, most of them in their early twenties. They are painting schools and public buildings throughout the Republic, they are carving doors and friezes, they are making woodcuts and illustrating books, they are modeling heads of Lenin and Madero, and they are designing and executing heroic statues in all the important cities of the land. But one cannot escape the thought that the technique of Revolutionary art in Mexico is fixed, that the characters have become stereotyped, and that methods have been standardized. The young men are already beginning to do better murals than Rivera and Orozco; but they are improving the molds, not making new ones. The author visited Pacheco and Uguarte on their scaffolds in the National Normal School during the summer of 1937. Their work is superb in coloring and craftsmanship, it appears definitely superior to that of Orozco and Rivera, there is sincerity and soul in the fresco; but it is definitely becoming "school."

[24] Luis Cardoza y Aragon, *loc cit.*

FUNCTIONAL ARCHITECTURE IN MEXICO

Few things influence the thinking of a people more than the architecture about them. The Englishman is unquestionably more conservative than the American, and this tendency may perhaps be traced as definitely to the hoary edifices about him as to any other single factor. The Chinese have been held in their thought orbits for thousands of years by the sight of ancient temple and pagoda. Because of this natural law, a corollary would be that one of the surest methods of changing the thinking of a people is to change their architecture. Such a beginning has been made in Mexico, and one of the most significant and telling of the methods of indoctrination is the building of modern schools of the "functional" type. This architecture is a natural outgrowth of the artistic theories of the Syndicate, with its demand for the indigenous and the useful.

The rise of functionalism is, in a way, a negation of the dogma of the Revolutionaries that private business makes no contribution to culture or civilization. One of the chief midwives at the birth of functional architecture was Sánchez Fogarty, sales promoter for the Tolteca Cement Company. He flooded Mexico with the *Revista Tolteca,* which promoted competitions in the field of building design. José Villagrán García, a young architect, collated the elements scattered by the artist and Fogarty, and became the pioneer of a new type of construction. As its name suggests, functional architecture stripped off the gingerbread and gewgaws of the baroque, churrigeresque, plateresque, and rococo.

Of all the habiliments of an artificial civilization the architectural dress of seventeenth-, eighteenth-, and nineteenth-century Mexico is perhaps the most factitious. No matter how exaggerated a country's architecture may be, there is usually a reason for it: China's upward curving eaves are to pitch demons, who would slide earthward, into the air once more. The most imposing Gothic castle was built for actual defense. But Mexican buildings of the Spanish and early independence era had no excuse whatever for their grotesquerie; they were simply European copies. Fogarty wanted cement used, and encouraged its use wherever possible. As it is difficult to make fancy concrete edifices, concrete buildings tended to become plain. García took advantage of this plainness and designed buildings that had a maximum of utility. A premium was placed on floor space, window area, with increased light and air, and simple corners and angles that could be kept clean.

In 1926 García was invited to teach architecture at the National Academy. Here he soon gathered a group of young men, who spread the gospel of functionalism to the corners of Mexico during the next few years. Juan O'Gorman, Enrique del Moral, Mauricio Campos, Alvaro Aburto, Leonardo Noriega, Salvador Roncal, Francisco Arce, Jesus Robado, Javier Torres Ansorena, and Carlos Vergara were among his students. Since 1926 these men have built hospitals, office buildings, workers' residences and apartments, residences, and, above all, schools. Juan O'Gorman and Juan Legarreta have been the outstanding members of the group, Legarreta designed a minimum house for laborers that was approved by the Departamento Central and was later built in large numbers. O'Gorman received a commission at one time to design almost one hundred and fifty more. Everywhere one goes in Mexico City and in the other large urban centers he sees ultramodern buildings. This trend is especially true in school construction. The Central School of the Revolution, built on the site of the infamous Carcel de Belem, a brutal Colonial prison, is an example of the beauty of simplicity

and utility. The four stories are of unornamented, rein-
forced concrete. Every room in the tremendous edifice,
which now has a coeducational student body of five thousand, is accessible to air and sunshine.

Like every other movement in modern Mexico this renaissance has often been challenged. According to one
authority,

This opposition is principally due, I am convinced, to a reactionary group who have consistently and loudly opposed every
move of innovation or progress in the last two decades, ranging from the agrarian reforms to the music and conduction of
Carlos Chavez.[25]

Nevertheless, buildings have been erected in the modern
manner and more are being erected. Many are decorated
with murals inside; many have suggestive sculptures near
the front or on the façade. Mexico has ever been a country of monuments; and today there are, radiating from
the Monument of the Revolution to the frontiers of the
nation, statues and memorials to the heroes and ideals of
the Revolution. All the edifices designed are expected to
condition the thinking of the millions who pass them daily.
In the words of José Villagrán García they are expected
to "(1) set forth reluctantly and to make known the pe-
culiarities of our people, and (2) take an active and leading part in the evolution of our people."[26]

ART IN THE SCHOOLS

Art pedagogy has experienced the same evolution as
other forms of thought since the days of 1921. Undirected
expression is no longer the keynote of the classroom or
salon. There must now be a definite social ideology behind
the work of each student. The artist is not considered in

[25] Beach Riley, "Social Progress and the New Architecture,"
Architectural Record, April 1937, p. 18.   [26] *Ibid.*, p. 32.

the light in which he has shone in Europe and America for so long. No longer is he a superman, a superindividualist; he is simply a workman, the same as a mason or a shoemaker. It is recognized that he has an individual ability that all men do not have but that that ability is to be placed at the disposal of society, just as the superior strength of a longshoreman is to be used for the common good.

Art is no longer considered a cloistered activity that flourishes in an ivory tower; it is rather a social force and as such is to be taught:

Quiere decir esto, que el arte no siempre vive en una situación, ideal y extrasocial, el artista no es un ser diferente en nada del hombre común, lo único que diferencia al artista del hombre común, es que su especialidad es el arte, un medio de trabajo como cualquiera otro.[27]

With this theory in mind, Mexico's art teachers encourage their students, from the *jardín de niños* upward, to gain an individual ideology and express it artistically. There is no painting of pictures for the mere technical training or to express some individual whim or mood unless it has social significance. As it is difficult to express an idea fully in a single scene, the work in the primary schools is tending more and more to two or more successive scenes.

The child may take any of the phases of the government reform to pictorialize. If he feels strongly about drunkenness, he may show a man receiving his pay envelope, going to the *cantina* or *pulquería*, drinking, and later fighting and ending in jail. To make it more graphic, other scenes may be added in which the drunkard's family is shown hungry, poorly clothed, and ill-sheltered. Collective bargaining comes in for considerable treatment; workers are shown being belabored by company guards

[27] Angel E. Salas, *Arte y Literatura Proletarios*, p. 8.

or police, while a corresponding number, well organized and carrying placards, are able to defy the exploiting class. Zapata is a well-liked figure among school children as well as among older Mexican painters. Cleanliness furnishes material for many infantile works of art; the advisability of boiling drinking water, the importance of typhoid inoculations and smallpox vaccinations, and the value of regular savings come in for much esthetic treatment.

Anti-imperialism and anti-Fascism have proved immensely popular among the embryo artists who have more violent natures and demand a stronger expression. When treating these two subjects no artistic restraint is practiced, and the bitterest form of graphic invective is permitted. Original work is often supplemented by pictures clipped from newspapers. To the pictorial display they add slogans and caricatures of their own composition.

Posters and newspaper murals are made up in schools all over the nation, the newspaper mural taking the place of the school paper in the United States. In some schools the entire presentation is pictorial and highly ideological; in other cases it may be made up of printed material ranging from school news to the war in Europe. In general there is a strong editorial on some stock subject. The making of the newspaper mural is a class project and usually requires a week to produce. It comes out on a regular date as does a newspaper.

The comic strip is used more and more extensively by the various departments of the Secretariat. For instance, the *Gráfico de Agricultura* carries on the back page of its weekly edition for elementary schools the comic doings of Polin and Pilon. Pilon is a typical *campesino* of the old school, ignorant and superstitious; Polin knows the scientific facts of farm life. Their weekly adventures are entertaining and enlightening.

Chapter V

REVOLUTIONARY MUSIC AND DANCING

Music and dancing play a unique role in Mexico's socialistic education. They are not mere subjects used to fill out the school program; they are rather key activities around which the school life is built. Singing is recognized the world over as a morale builder. Mexican leaders expect it to serve the function of Mexicanizing the nation, of giving it an esprit de corps. Dancing is a group activity par excellence for teaching the individual to lose himself in the communal spirit. He is en rapport with society so completely that his individual will is merged into that of the common will and he is, for the nonce, acting harmoniously as a smoothly functioning unit of a large social body. Music and dancing are in the programs of every school in the country, while mathematics and writing are not.

AIMS OF REVOLUTIONARY MUSIC AND DANCING

The meaning of the term *revolucionario* needs to be restated occasionally in order to keep its connotation clear. *Revolucionario,* in the Mexican sociological usage, is not synonymous with the English word "revolutionary." The word *revolucionario* is a shibboleth; it is used to test all material in the school program to see that it is not traditional and that it is in accord with the proletarian school.

Los programas del tipo revolucionario son los que no toman en cuenta nada de lo establecido en programas anteriores, tienden a crear, a investigar, a huir de toda tradición y estudiar, en cambio, el material vivo, en el niño y sus intereses.[1]

Revolutionary education is, in short, the child-centered school.

There is little if any of the swashbuckling, martial type of music in the collections that are being used throughout Mexico. It must be kept in mind that Socialism is a philosophy of love and peace; therefore the music glorifies these concepts, as well as useful work, nature, and the individual. Music in the school is primarily aiding Socialism to unify the nation, not to disrupt it.

Ahora debemos poner el canto al servicio de las ideas socialistas y enseñar canciones verdaderamente revolucionarias y en último caso, producciones que enseñen algo util y efectivo.[2]

Revolutionary music, therefore, has a definitely constructive place in the educational scheme. It does not aim to foment hatred against the wealthy classes or against foreign countries. Rather, it aims to restore dignity to the Mexican and his country and customs. It aims to undo the work of European music in Mexico which has tended to glorify the culture of Europe and to depreciate that of indigenous Mexico. In addition, Revolutionary music tends to have a moralizing influence: it gets the folk away from the *cantinas* and *pulquerías*, traditional centers of debasing escapism, and gives them new cultural and esthetic centers. It is in accord with the Socialist's philosophic concept of developing the *ser plenario*.

---

[1] Victor M. Reyes, "La Jugueteria Hecha por los Niños Mexicanos," *Revista de Educación*, Diciembre de 1937.

[2] José Teran Tovar, "La Enseñanza del Canto," *El Maestro Rural*, Enero de 1936.

La propaganda tenía dos fines, uno artístico de difundir el gusto por la musica en el pueblo, y otro moralizador, de apartar al pueblo de los lugares de disipación dándole centro de reunión y socialbilidad para que hallara en la música solaz y honesto entretenimiento.[3]

Accord of revolutionary music with Socialist philosophy.—The prime characteristic of Socialist education, that it shall be indigenous, and that it shall fit the people and the locale, is especially true of the renascent music of Mexico. The present music goes back to the pre-Cortesian music of the country and to the submerged music of the people that has been completely ignored by Mexican composers for four hundred years. As the Revolution was a popular movement, an uprising of the people, they expressed themselves during the Revolution with great gusto through their own songs.

The first and most typical expression of native art was the spontaneous adoption of Mexican tunes as the campaign songs of the Revolution. The agrarians under Zapata marched to the simple refrain of "Adelita." Villa's guerrillas raided to the rhythmic tune of "La Cucaracha." The catching simplicity of "Valentina" was endeared to the followers of Carranza. Calles adopted "La Borrachita" as his 1924 political campaign song. Music was in the soul of the Mexican and, in the newly found freedom by revolution, he turned to native tunes for an overt manifestation of joy. The peasants' humble melodies became fashionable. They were of the people and by the people, and in proletarian revolutionary Mexico, they received popular acclaim.[4]

With all Mexicans singing songs about their own country and the simple things and persons of that country, the composers turned astonished eyes upon their own music and really discovered it for the first time. They discovered

[3] Ruben Campos, *El Folklore y la Musica Mexicana,* p. 151.

[4] George I. Sanchez, *Mexico: A Revolution by Education* (The Viking Press, 1936), p. 59.

that Mexico is perhaps the richest country in the world for musical appreciation and for musical background. It dawned upon the Revolutionaries that they did not need to import Revolutionary songs from France and Russia and thus perpetuate the tradition of imposing foreign customs on the people.

As post-Revolutionary Mexico began to study the music of the people she found that what had been true of art was true of music. The music and the dance, as they flourished among the people, came almost directly from the indigenous music of the autochthons of the country. True, they had been influenced by European music; but the vigorous body came directly from the pre-Cortesian Indians. Immediately the Revolutionary musicians began a study of *mestizo* music that led them to its beginning—indigenous music.

The Spaniards had done such a thorough job of stamping out all record of and all respect for the indigenous arts that much research had to be done to get at a knowledge of pre-Cortesian music and dancing. From the ancient musical instruments in the National Museum and from the written reports of a few early Church Fathers, notably Juan de Torquemada and Bernardino de Sahagun, it was possible to reconstruct the original musical heritage of Mexico. As usual, the Secretaria de Educación Pública took the lead in this musical renaissance by instituting the Dirección de Cultura Estética. Folk dances and songs were collected from all parts of the country, and every shred of knowledge concerning them collated. All of this information was incorporated by Ruben Campos in three monumental works: *El Folklore y la Música Mexicana* (1928), *El Folklore Literario de México* (1929), and *El Folklore Musical de las Ciudades* (1930). The National Conservatory of Music carried on an exhaustive study of pre-Cortesian musical instruments, publishing its findings in the review, *Music,* and in the annals of the National Museum.

The most significant findings of all this research were that indigenous music was tremendously Mexican and predominantly communal—two cardinal points of Scientific Socialism. Music was an integrated activity of the highest order among the Aztecs.

Music was played, sung, and danced simultaneously, in groups of various sizes, some of which, according to chroniclers, consisted of as many as several thousand persons. Little or nothing is known of the existence of an individual music used for the expression of the personal feelings of the artist. . . . . But no artistical musical expression, even though composed by a known individual, failed to be the expression of collective sentiment, for it was always the people in a group who sang, played, and danced for the satisfaction of a collective social necessity.[5]

1. *Indigenous Mexican music.*—Ancient Mexico was saturated with music and dancing.[6] The two great professions, religion and war, started and finished every activity with music. Every act had its own ritual, which was carried out to the throb of the *ahuehuetl* and the *teponaztli,* the carved drums of the Aztecs; the wail of the flute-like *tlapitzalli,* made from baked clay, or the *tzicahuaztli,* made from human bones; the rattle of gourds filled with pebbles; and the whistle of the *ateocolli,* made from seashells, or of the *chililihtli,* a small clay, high-pitched flute. The rhythms of the daily life, birth, death, and marriage, planting and harvesting, and festivals to the sun and rain gods were punctuated by music.

[5] Carlos Chavez, "Mexican Music," in *Renascent Mexico,* by Hubert Herring and Herbert Weinstock (Covici-Friede), pp. 202–3.

[6] Gabriel Salvidar, "El Origen de la Danza," *Nuestro Mexico,* Julio de 1932.

Indigenous Mexican music is primarily rhythmic. It lacks the melody of European music, because there were but five notes in its musical scale. The nature of the instruments, percussion and wind, and the fact that the music was designed chiefly for dancing, gave it a strongly marked accent that is still evident in Mexican music. The words used to carry out the love of rhythm were childlike in meter and choice of words. Many of the verses are almost pure onomatopoeia. Campos gives an example that is beautifully primitive in its inception. It is the "Peregrination of Aztlan," and is based on the legend that a sacred bird told the ancient Aztecs to move on and so caused them to wander on to Tenochtitlan. The music and the words are inspired by the song and twitter of the bird. In Nahuatl, *Tihui* means "Let us go."

TIHUI

Aztatzitzintin ti, tin, tin tin, tin.
Tihui, tihuiyan, tihui, tihui,
Tihui, tihuiyan, tihui, tihui,
Aztatzitzintin ti, tin, tin. tin.[7]

This same love of primitive meter is evident in the Dance of the Little Indians, even after it has been translated into Spanish. Although this fiesta is the second most popular in Mexico, the words have little significance, merely furnishing a background patter for the dance. One stanza will serve for illustration:

[7] Ruben Campos, *op. cit.*, p. 37.

Agua lica, ni canca sonaja.
Agua lica, ni canca catera.
Mi tonche mi lonche,
Mi malacatonche
Con la melcochera..

Y Santo "Siñor de Chalma"
Pititun, pititun, tun tun.[8]

This music is a part of Mexico. It is inspired by the birds and beasts of her countryside, it is as harsh as her precipitous mountains and as haunting as the perfume of her spring flowers. Modern Mexican composers are turning to it daily for a sincere music that will at the same time be inspired by Mexico and help to weld a soul for the nation. Carlos Chavez, one of the leading composers and musicians of today, owes his new vision to early contact with indigenous music. He lived for years near Tlascala, where the sterile soil of the mountains had kept out foreigners and the culture had remained practically unchanged. As he continued to study Europeanized Mexican music he constantly thought of the haunting, vigorous music of his own people, until he was influenced to a return to the music of Mexico.

This music of *huehuetl, chirimía,* flutes and drums is purely traditional and indigenous : rhythmic, contrapuntal, vigorous, of astonishing vigor and conviction. Whenever I heard this music I was gripped by its force, by its unlimited command. It has never, in later periods when I was subjected to varied influences, ceased to be for me the most important formative element.[9]

2. *Mestizo music.*—The Church stamped out much of the music and many of the ritual dances, such as it could not eradicate being adapted to Catholic purposes.[10] Each

---

[8] Secretaria de Educación Pública, *Los Inditos.*
[9] Carlos Chavez, *Renascent Mexico* (Covici-Friede), p. 211.
[10] *Ibid.;* also Erna Fergusson, *Fiesta in Mexico,* 10 ff.

year the Indians return to the hill of Tepeyac and dance
the pagan dances at the shrine of the Virgin of Guadalupe
as they have done for centuries. The Dance of Los Inditos
is now danced for Our Lord of Chalma as it was formerly
danced for Oztocteotl, God of the Caves.[11] The *jarabe,*
considered the national dance of Mexico, was among those
that were frowned upon by the authorities. In 1802 Don
Felix Berenger banned the *jarabe,* declaring that anyone
dancing it should be imprisoned for two years, while on-
lookers should be sentenced to at least two months in jail.[12]
Under the Colonial régime and for the first century of independence it was considered vulgar to sing Indian songs
or indulge in regional dances.[13]

However, a new music appeared in Mexico which has
since come to be known as *mestizo* music. It is a fusion of
the indigenous music and the various European varieties
that have flourished in Mexico. Fray Pedro de Gante used
music extensively in his first school at Texcoco. He set
the names of saints to music and thus taught Spanish and
Church materials at the same time. The French and Italian influences have been marked in the musical tradition
of the nation. During the reign of Maximilian, Austrian
music made a brief appearance and its influence can still
be felt in such pieces as *"Sobre las Olas,"* "Over the
Waves," which was composed in honor of Carlota and is
reminiscent of Strauss.

The introduction of European musical instruments was
as influential in the growth of a *mestizo* music as any other
factor. The guitar was borrowed by the Spaniards from
the Arabs and given to Mexico, where it has found a

---

[11] This dance may be found in Norma Schwendener and Averil Tibbels, *Legends and Dances of Old Mexico,* p. 97.

[12] *Ibid.,* p. 3.

[13] Erna Fergusson, *Fiesta in Mexico,* p. 18.

REVOLUTIONARY MUSIC AND DANCING   121

definite place for itself. The same is true of the *chirimía,* a double-reed flute, probably borrowed from the Asturians, who developed it from the Roman *gaita.*[14] The violin is played all over Mexico in a way that Europeans never dreamed of:

> The natives of the States of Michoacan, Mexico, and Puebla principally, construct violins equal to, or resembling, those of Europe. Nevertheless, when we hear them in Mexican orchestras, they do not seem to remind us of their conventional style, as much because of the special materials of their construction as because of the manner of playing them and the kinds of music played.[15]

It is this very originality of treatment and handling of European materials that has made *mestizo* music typically Mexican.

As the music subtly changed its nature after its admixture of European melody, so did the dance; for in Mexico one hardly speaks of the two separately. Dances are spoken of in Mexico as *zapateados,* from the infinitive, *zapatear,* to tap the time or click the measure with shoes, *zapatos.* All of the best-known dances originated in Spain, but the way they are now danced makes them definitely Mexican.

> The Indian influence is shown in the pose of the upper body, different in every dance and typical of the gait and movement of each region, and in a certain dignity and poise which make the dances truly Mexican and not Spanish.[16]

The *jarabe tapatio,* of Jalisco, the *huapango* from Vera Cruz, the *sandunga* of Tehuantepec, and the *jarana* of Yucatan are the outstanding regional dances of Mexico. The music for the *jarabe* is furnished by stringed instruments, usually the *mariachi* or *vihuela,* a Mexican development of

[14] Carlos Chavez, *Renascent Mexico* (Covici-Friede), p. 213.
[15] *Ibid.,* pp. 212–13.
[16] Erna Fergusson, *Fiesta in Mexico* (Alfred A. Knopf), p. 19.

the guitar. *Mariachi* bands as a rule consist of violin, *mariachi*, and any other local instrument available. What is lacked in instrumentation is furnished by the shrill falsetto whoop of the Mexican singer. Typical *mariachi* music defies musicians; but its lively, rapidly changing time is ideally suited to the temperament of the Mexican and his dances.[17]

The *Danza de los Viejitos,* "Dance of the Little Old Men," also comes from Jalisco and is one of the few comic dances of the nation. The dancers wear masks representing old men and carry canes with which they tap out a quick, moving measure. *Los tecomates* is the gourd dance, as its name implies. Gourds are used for ornamentation and to add to the rhythm of the dance. *Las sembradoras* is a dance dedicated to the sowers of crops. It is danced on the second of February and is a dance of thanksgiving. Farm animals, corn, wheat, and other products of the harvest are gaily added to the background of the performance. *Los negritos* and *los moros* are beautiful old dances particularly favored in the Lake Patzcuaro region of Michoacan. Both are colorful and almost ritualistic in execution.

La virgen y las fieras,[18] "The Virgin and the Beasts," is a dance based on an old Indian legend: A beautiful girl lived near a dark forest. All the animals in the forest loved the sweet, kindly girl. One day she strayed far into the forest and the evil spirits attacked her. The beasts formed a cordon about her and thus saved her from the forces of evil.

The Yaqui deer dance is a ceremonial movement in which the hunter pursues the deer about a fire. Both are

[17] Elena Picazo de Murray and Paul V. Murray, "The Charm of Mexico's Popular Music," *Étude,* August 1937.

[18] *El jarabe, huapango, los viejitos, los tecomates; las sembradoras, los negritos, los moros, and la virgen y las fieras* are described in detail by Schwendener and Tibbels, *Legends and Dances of Old Mexico.*

masked and wear gourds about their ankles which give out a constant rattle during the dance. *Las canacuas* is a dance of Michoacan which symbolizes the hospitality of the Tarascan Indians. This dance is highly colorful, as it allows the display of the picturesque costumes of the Tarascans as well as a showing of the handsomely carved and lacquered wooden trays of the region, known as *jícaras*. The dance is accompanied by the singing of "Jícaras de Michoacan." This song is such an excellent example of what the modern Mexicans consider worth while that it is included here. It has beauty of word and movement and glorifies the artifacts that are truly Mexican.

Jícaras, jícaras, jícaras de Michoacán,
donde el alma de un artista
puso en su arte loco afán.
Pájaros, flores, fantasías del amor
están en ellas combinados
en armónico color.

Chorus
Tierra de flores, de bellos paisajes,
de lagos azules, y espléndido sol;
O tierra de ensueños, jamás te he olvidado,
eres el anhelo de mi corazón.[19]

From the background of these dances and many others that have been danced all over Mexico, the Department of Education is compiling, describing, and disseminating dance information and dance consciousness to the people.

The School of the Dance of the Department of Education is already using themes, steps, music and costumes taken from both secular and ritual dances, and adapting them to the stage. The first experiments have been both very Mexican and exceedingly beautiful.[20]

[19] Edith Johnston, *Regional Dances of Mexico* (Banks Upshaw and Company, Dallas, Texas), p. 31.

[20] Erna Fergusson, *Fiesta in Mexico* (Alfred A. Knopf), p. 27.

Certainly there is no question but that the dance and the music being propagated through the work of the schools is truly national, truly Mexican, and thus fulfills the prime tenet of the Socialist schools: The school shall be Mexican.

THE TEACHING OF REVOLUTIONARY MUSIC

In the schools of Mexico the aim is to have trained music teachers for all the schools, if possible. At present the majority of the schools have no special teacher, the general-purpose *maestro* teaching music with his other duties. A period is set aside for singing and is preceded and followed by a rest period.

Special care is taken that the children shall not strain their voices. They are not allowed to sing too loud or to make harsh, unpleasant noises. In the kindergarten simple songs are used, often songs of only three notes. In the elementary grades more advanced songs are sung. Care is always taken with diction and with understanding the meaning of the words.

Spanish teaching is a natural by-product of music instruction. Among the Indians music is the most useful subject in the school for language instruction. The natural interests of the child are considered, too, in the choice of songs. In the first and second grades the teacher selects songs having to do with birds, animals, and nature. In the third and fourth grades there are songs of trips and adventures. Romance and sentiment are introduced into the music used in the fifth and sixth grades. Care is always exercised, however, that the songs of sentiment shall be simple, pure, and true to nature and shall not border on the erotic. The adventures and struggles must not be of the type in which strength exploits weakness.[21]

Singing is almost entirely a group activity. The class

[21] José Teran Tovar, *loc. cit.*

LA CANASTA

Traigo mi ca-nas-ta llena de con-fi-tes te que-das-te
so-la por-que tú qui-sis-te. To-ma_esta canas-ti-ta de chi-les
ver-des quien te manda ser bu-rro por-que no muer-des.

is trained to sing as a unit, with careful selection according to voices and parts. Whenever possible the group sings in the open air, and always with the members standing. In the late afternoon the adults come to the school when they have finished their day's work. Instrumental music and group singing for all often lasts into the evening. *Orfeones,* Orpheus clubs, have been started all over Mexico for various adult groups. The purpose is to build up singing units in factories, guilds, and communities. The army is also given regular training in group singing, and on various occasions large army units have sung publicly with great effectiveness. In 1927 a concourse of fifteen thousand children from the elementary schools gave a mass concert in the National Stadium of Mexico City.

A series of musical extravaganzas has been presented throughout Mexico from 1923 up to the present time to further the work of cultural propaganda. *Las Canacuas* was played in the mountain village of Paracho, Michoacan, in 1923. This musical ballet presented the musical history of Mexico. Part One consisted of music and dances composed or popular around the year 1870. Part Two was reduced to indigenous songs played on the *chirimía, teponaztli,* and *tambor.* Parts Three and Four presented music from the Maya and Isthmus of Tehuantepec regions.

In 1925 a pantomine with a colorful musical background was presented at the open-air theater of San Juan Teotíhuacan. This pantomine, called *Tlahuicole,* unfolded the legend of a famous Tlascalan gladiator who defeated all adversaries sent against him in the ancient contests which preceded the Aztec religious rites. Thousands of persons came from all parts of Mexico and many from abroad to see this masterpiece, which was later shown in the patio of the Secretariat of Education.[22] In 1929 *El*

22 Ruben M. Campos, *El Folklore Musical de los Ciudades,* p. 200.

Laborillo was offered in Oaxaca, one of Mexico's richest sections for folklore, and was later shown in the Workers' Park of Balbuena in Mexico City.

The ballet *Quetzalcoatl* is considered by Mexican authorities to be the apotheosis of the modern Revolutionary spirit of art.[23] The painter Carlos Gonzalez designed the setting and costumes, while Alberto Flachebba collated and composed a musical score. The ancient Aztec religious capital Tollan, or Tula, as it is called today, furnished the setting for this epic of the bearded god-king. Dancing, color, music and movement blended to produce a spiritual catharsis that was truly Mexican in nature, truly Revolutionary:

... es la fusión de todos los ritmos, de todos los sonidos, de todos los colores y de todos los movimientos en una fiesta de poesia, en un embrujamiento de color, en un extasis de espiritualidad. Su desbordamiento de vida viola todos los preceptos establecidos, porque es una manifestación artística revolucionaria, que reclama para el arte representativo y plastico una amplitud como jamás la ha tenido ninguna otra.[24]

Other spectacles have been presented and are still being presented throughout the Republic. *Sacnicte, Xochitl, Coosiheuza y Moctezuma Xocoyotzin, La Fiesta de Tlaloc,* and *Anahuac* are in the growing repertoire of the Secretariat of Education. Each one is presented in its proper geographical setting and serves the double purpose of teaching local history to the people and building up pride of self, race, and country.

MATERIALS OF REVOLUTIONARY MUSIC

Perhaps the most popular type of song in Mexico is the *corrido,* distantly akin to the English ballad in form but with the important exception that the *corrido* has to do

[23] *Ibid.,* p. 202.　　　　[24] *Ibid.,* p. 202.

"LA MANZANA CHATA"

Són Michoacano   **Recop. Roberto.Angeles**

Tempo di Vals

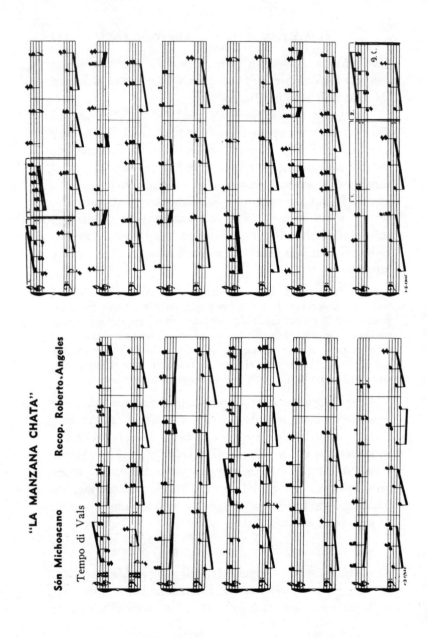

VIDA RANCHERA

Huapango Chiapaneco   Recop. J. Jesús G. Gaona

with current happenings. It is usually a long, narrative poem depending on apostrophe and irony at times. The *corrido* is particularly well adapted to the work of propaganda, for it uses descriptive adjectives with pithiness and telling effect. There is a body of folk poetry in existence that details every happening from the coming of the Spaniard to the adoption of the *plan sexenal*. The *son* is another typical Mexican musical form. *Sones* are the tunes that accompany *jarabes,* and the words that go with the *sones* are truly folklore. They are simple in arrangement and the vocabulary is of the people, describing things they know.

To know the Mexican people one should be familiar with its songs. For not only the music is significant, in its variations from the little more than rhythmic monotone among the less developed indigenous groups to the sophisticated syncopations of the capital : The words of the songs reveal much that is expressed in no other way.[25]

A few stanzas of typical *corridos* and folksongs will give an indication of the nature of the music being sung all over Mexico, both in the school and out. Since English translations lose the flavor and swing of the Mexican originals, most of the examples given are in the Spanish. *La Valentina* still tinkles from the guitars of Mexican musicians as it did when the followers of Carranza swung along to its cadence :

> Una pasión me domina,
> es la que me ha hecho venir.
> Valentina, Valentina,
> yo te quisiera decir.
>
> Que por esos tus amores
> La vida voy a perder;

[25] Ernest Gruening, *Mexico and Its Heritage* (D. Appleton-Century Company), p. 647.

si me han de matar mañana
que me maten de una vez.[26]

So, for many stanzas, continues the plaint of the soldier.
Zapata is memorialized thus:

Harken, educated public; to the song about our martyr,
Verses telling you the story of Emiliano Zapata,
Of his taking up of arms, and to fight then like a hero,
To defend the noble cause of Francisco I. Madero.

On the twentieth of November when the war blazed up in ter-
    ror,
Was Madero in San Luis, and Zapata in his *tierra;*
And Zapata helped Madero, helped him to achieve a victory,
Feeling that the plans of each contained nothing contradictory.

But, no land was being given; "And if now Madero fail us,
We'll fight on," declared Zapata, "we the people of Morelos,
We, the suffering *campesinos,* who have lived till now in
    squalor,"
And he thereupon proclaimed revolt—the Plan of Villa
Ayala.[27]

Zapata as a symbol embodies the group consciousness
of the Indians of Morelos which developed during the
Revolution. His exploits are sung all over Mexico, but it
is especially in Morelos that his memory is revered. *Corridos* about him, written elsewhere in Mexico, describe his
"base passions" and refer to him as "an Attila." But in
the songs of the local collection he is "our defender," "a
Napoleon," "our exalted savior," "the scourge of many a
traitor," and "so wise and quick-thinking a *veterano.*"

Les encargó a las fuerzas surianas
    Que como jefe y sublime redentor;
Su memoria conserven mañana
    Como prueba de su patria amor.

[26] "Canciones Revolucionarias," *Nuestro Mexico,* Noviembre 1932.
[27] From Ernest Gruening, *Mexico and Its Heritage* (D. Appleton-
Century Company), p. 648.

SAN MIGUEL TZITZIKI

FLOR DE CANELA

"He charged the forces of the south
As chief and exalted savior;
To preserve his memory tomorrow
As a proof of their love of country."[28]

In his guerrilla warfare Zapata and his raiders sang the simple "Adelita" which is still heard in Morelos and the other states of Mexico:

Adelita se llama la joven
a quien quiero y no puedo olvidar,
a quien amo e idolatro,
y con quien me voy a casar.

Sí, Adelita, has de ser mi esposa,
sí, Adelita, seras mi mujer
coloca en tu pecho esta rosa
y te llevo a bailar al cuartel.[29]

Villa, too, has his place in the folk music of the country, but his niche is not the same as that of Zapata. He is the picaresque, roistering type; he is *muy hombre,* an adventurer with the ladies and a daredevil in war. The following *corrido*[30] exemplifies his derring-do in warfare:

THE TAKING OF ZACATECAS BY VILLA, URBINA, AND NATERA

Hah! You drunkard Victoriano,
Your bad heart will slip a beat,
When you hear of Zacatecas
Where your troops have met defeat.

On the twenty-third of June—
I address those who are here,
"Pancho" Villa stormed the city,
Taking it by front and rear.

[28] Robert Redfield, *Tepoztlán, A Mexican Village* (The University of Chicago Press), p. 199.

[29] "Canciones Revolucionarias," *Nuestro Mexico,* Noviembre 1932.

[30] Ernest Gruening, *op. cit.,* p. 648.

All the streets of Zacatecas
Were piled high with federal dead,
And the few that were not slaughtered,
Early in the day had fled.

For some federals were so frightened,
That they hid in women's skirts,
Pulling them up over trousers,
And mantillas over shirts.

The difference in the underlying motives of the Revo-
lutionary leaders is exactly portrayed by the mood and
tone of their marching songs. *"La Cucaracha,"* "The
Cockroach," is the gayest, most rollicking, most devil-
may-care of the songs to come out of the Revolution.
Carranza, the arch-enemy of Villa, is characterized as the
cockroach, and most of the stanzas of the interminable
Cucaracha are lusty and bawdy. *Cucaracha* swept the
United States after its popularization in the cinema, "Viva
Villa." One stanza will show the spirit and movement of
this song:

LA CUCARACHA

Un panadero fue a misa,
No encontrando que rezar,
Le pidio a la virgen pura,
Dinero para gastar.
(Repeat)

La Cucaracha, la cucaracha,
ya no puede caminar,
porque no tiene, porque la falta,
marihuana que fumar.
(Repeat)

The regional and folk music of Mexico which is being
gathered and disseminated so carefully is based on the
simplest of subjects. Any object in the daily life of the
Mexican may be the inspiration for a cameo-like song.

AMADRUS, SEÑORES

Andantino

A - ma - drus se - ño - res, ven - go de la Ha - ba - na,

de cor - tar ma - dro - ños pa - ra do - ña Jua - na.

La ma - no de - re - cha y des - pués la iz - quier - da

y des - pués de la - - do y des - pués cos - ta - do

un - na me - dia vuel - ta   con su re - ve - ren - cía tin -

tán llaman a la puer - ta tin - tán yo no quiero a - brír   tin -

tán que viene por - tí.

Experiences and daily routines are duly immortalized in *sones* about which dances are woven. The underlying moods behind these songs come from a variety of sources: The plaintive melancholy that underlies some of the music is traced to the Italian influence that swept Mexico in the first third of the nineteenth century;[31] the love songs that continually recur to the themes of *"amor," "de mi corazon,"* and *"de sus ojos negros,"* come from the Moorish influence on Spain; the strongly accented music that causes the hearer to *zapatear* in spite of himself is the indigenous contribution. The work of the schools in presenting this music as a unified whole is drawing the attention of musical experts from all of the Americas.

The schools are unusually progressive along these lines, and almost all of them devote a good deal of time to intelligent musical study.[32]

Post-Revolutionary songs have combined all the elements of the past to produce a music that is being felt strongly in the United States. Perhaps the one song that best expresses the sadness of the Mexican at the rape of his country by the warring forces of the Revolution is *"Las Cuatro Milpas," "The Four Cornfields"*:

Cuatro milpas tan solo han quedado
en el rancho que era mio. ... Ay!
Aquella casita tan blanca y bonita qué triste quedó.
Y por eso estoy triste, morena
Y por eso me pongo, y me pongo a llorar,
recordando las horas felices
que juntos pasamos in mi dulce hogar.
    Los potreros están sin ganado
toditito se ha acabado, ay ...
Y ya no hay palomas, ni flores, ni aromas todo se acabo.

[31] Elena Picazo de Murray and Paul V. Murray, *loc. cit.*
[32] Verna Arvey, "Mexico's Significance in Present Day Music," *Étude*, February 1936.

Another song that has come out of Mexico to achieve popularity in the United States also glorifies the *rancho*: *"Allá en el Rancho Grande."* This is a gay tune that quite forgets the scorched ranch houses and the dead cattle. Both of these songs were used in moving pictures bearing the same names as the songs. Another regional song that takes the everyday joys and sorrows of ranch life as its theme is called simply *"Vida Ranchera."* This is a *huapango* from Chiapas. *"La Canasta"* is a bit of music based on a basket full of green peppers. The golden oranges of Mexico are immortalized in a simple, childish tune, *"Naranja dulce, limón partida."* A *son* that is much used in the lower grades for singing and dancing shows the Indian love of strongly accented rhythm, *"La Pájara Pinta,"* "The Colored Bird."

> Estaba la pájara pinta
> a la sombra del verde limón.
> Con el pico, picaba la rama,
> con la cola movía la flor.
> ¡Ay! sí! ¡ay! no, ¿cuándo vendrá mi amor?[33]

The hawk, the snake, and even the dog form the basis for these regional songs. The names of many fruits and vegetables are more musical and exotic than in English, so that their sounds are pure poetry. In *"Las Cuatro Milpas"* the word *potrero* is poetical and musical, whereas its English equivalent, waterhole, loses that connotation. An example of the words plum, apricot, cantaloupe, and watermelon being blended into poetry comes from *"A La Vibora, Vibora"*:

> —Una mexicana que fruta vendia,
> ciruelas, chabacanos,
> melon o sandia ... tras, tras.[34]

---

[33] Luis F. Obregon, *Recreación Física*, p. 36.
[34] *Ibid.*, p. 39.

Perhaps the epitome of this type of music is *"El Zopilote,"* "The Buzzard." A gay, regional song comes from the state of Guerrero telling of the search by the little buzzard for a mate to console him.

> Este es el zopilotito de Ayahualco de Guerrero
> que lo mero Zuni, zuni, zuni lo zopilotito.[35]

The musical names of flowers are not overlooked in these songs. In *"Milano"*—

> —Vamos a la huerta,
> de toro, toronjil,
> a ver a "Milano"
> comiendo perejil.
> —Milano no está aquí
> está en su vergel,
> abriendo la rosa
> y cerrando el clavel.[36]

"Yanqui Jazz" is reviled and inveighed against by music leaders, but it is definitely a factor that must be considered. American films and records are popular all over Mexico. To hear a *mariachi* orchestra playing a popular composition from the United States is a marvel never to be forgotten. Agustín Lara, one of the most prolific composers of popular music, combines all the foreign and native elements that go into the making of Mexican music but still has his feet on Mexican soil.

Agustín Lara was born in Vera Cruz and is the local hero. At least every other person with whom I talked asked me if I knew his song, Las Palmeras. And as we watched the trees against the sky we could see where he got the idea of palms drunk with the sun.[37]

[35] Secretaria de Educación Pública, *Música Regional Mexicana.*

[36] Luis F. Obregon, *op. cit.,* p. 41.

[37] Bess Adams Garner, *Mexico: Notes in the Margin* (Houghton Mifflin Company), p. 112.

LAS PALMERAS

Hay en tus ojos el verde esmeralda
que brota del mar,
Y en tu boquita la sangre marchita
que tiene el coral,
En las cadencias de tu voz divina
la rima de amor,
Y en tus ojeras se ven las palmeras
borrachas de sol.

From this brief review of Revolutionary music it is easy to see that music is one of the most potent of the tools of Socialism in Mexico. A full repertoire of Revolutionary music deepens the pride and belief of the Mexican both in himself and in his country. It gives an outlet for his innate esthetic senses, allowing for both creation and expression. Above all, it tends to blend the disparate elements of the country into a socialized, Mexicanized whole.

Chapter VI

CARRYING SOCIALISM TO THE PEOPLE

THE MORE fixed educational channels of Socialist indoctrination have been examined at some length. The institutions for that purpose include various types of schools, where the people, both children and adults, come to learn; mural and other forms of art that catch the eye of the passing Mexican; and music and dancing, as practiced by groups under Socialist teachers. All these forms of education do their part in guiding the thinking of groups in more settled parts of the country. But what of the *indio* who lives far back in the mountains, of the factory worker who toils from daylight to dark and has no opportunity to go near the cultural centers? What of the poverty-ridden stretches far from the capital where only a poor school is maintained by an almost illiterate teacher? How are these people to be reached with the message that Mexico's leaders consider so vital? Many techniques are employed to reach them, but the most important from the point of view of effectiveness and extensiveness are the Cultural Missions and the Centers of Indian Education.

THE CULTURAL MISSIONS

The Cultural Mission was distinctly the answer to a felt need when it first came into being in 1922. José Vasconcelos was then attacking the titanic work of building an educational system from scratch, with everything—plant, personnel, and techniques—to be developed. The people were demanding, pleading for, almost fighting for schools. Schools were being started in the most available buildings or in structures co-operatively built by communities. Teachers were being hurriedly recruited from the locality and, usually, were barely able to read and write. This first great "push" was classed as a campaign against illiteracy—at that time standing at about ninety per cent in Mexico. A renaissance as to mere reading and writing swept the country. Practically all observers mention classes that met in any kind of place available, including the middle of the street:

The campaign against illiteracy—planned as an auxiliary drive—brought forth many stirring examples of devotion. Equipment was lacking. In the patio of a *Casa de Vecindad* ("House of the Neighborhood") or tenement, I saw a girl of thirteen, who had gathered some twenty-five children about her, marking letters and figures on the pink-tinted plaster wall, while the mothers paused in their washing around the central stone fountain to gaze with admiration and awe. Another child of the same age, daughter of an illiterate plasterer, had taught her father and 150 children to read and write. These junior volunteer teachers were two out of several hundred drawn almost wholly from the laboring class.[1]

With a teaching staff made up of *misioneros*, volunteer teachers, who were in almost as great need of training as their students, it became imperative to furnish in-service training. The teacher needed help in meeting the problem of teaching classes of half-starved children. He needed help to build a school, to formulate a school program, and to start the work of community betterment.

[1] Ernest Gruening, *Mexico and Its Heritage* (D. Appleton-Century Company), p. 518.

It is of interest to note that the first Cultural Mission was under the direction of Rafael Ramírez, who later became Chief of the Department of Rural Education. This Mission established itself in Zacualtipan, Hidalgo, in the fall of 1923. In the faculty of the Mission were teachers of soap-making, tanning, health and physical education, agriculture, and music. Rural teachers from the surrounding region congregated for an institute, which included intensive training in the specialties and activities mentioned above as well as in the pedagogy of rural teaching and in Socialist orientation. Such worthwhile results were obtained, both in teacher training and in community betterment, that Señor Ramírez was asked to lead another Mission to Cuernavaca, Morelos, during the following year. After the first year's experience the institutes were held in small rural villages, where the environment was similar to that to which the teacher was accustomed, instead of in larger cities. The village was used as a laboratory for the teachers during the period of training. Men and women were organized into units of labor or peasant confederations, all inhabitants were vaccinated, and the young people were taught games and dances. Once the institute period was over, however, the village and school remained as a permanent center. Generally a model house was constructed, a library was established and soon used as the headquarters for other smaller libraries in the district, and the town remained as the site of the teachers' federation.

In planning the program of rural-teacher training in service, we have tried to keep in mind the following principles. First, training must be specific and intense ; second, the teacher should receive training in the technique of socialization both of the school and of the community.[2]

[2] Moisés Sáenz and H. I. Priestley, *Some Mexican Problems*, p. 80.

By the end of 1924 there were six Cultural Missions in the field. Since that time they have changed slightly in character because of changing conditions and increasing knowledge of the subject, but they have retained their most salient characteristic—their exploratory nature. A Bureau of Cultural Missions was established in 1926 with Señorita Elena Torres as its chief. The growth of the Missions may be shown by the following table:[3]

Year	Number of Missions	Institutes Held	Rural Teachers Attending	States Reached
1923	1	1	147	1
1926	6	42	2,327	11
1930	14	85	2,482	19
1935	18	75	4,494	20

Functional bases of the Cultural Missions.[4]—The primary purpose of the Cultural Mission is to better the primary school teacher, culturally and professionally, while he is in service. This betterment includes academic training and guidance in educational techniques. He is actually taught to read and write better, and is given further training in arithmetic, geography, and other subjects. The teacher is trained in education. He is given instruction in the science of education, educational psychology, school organization, methods of teaching, and group and committee organization. The technical training of the *maestro* is improved. He is taught the elements of scientific agriculture, care and feeding of animals, farm industries, and mechanics. Naturally this training, given in such a short time, will be of the most elementary type. However, the missioners believe that the mere teaching of the value of cultivation, irrigation, and rotation of

[3] George I. Sanchez, *Mexico: A Revolution by Education* (The Viking Press, 1936), p. 72.

[4] *Bases que Definen las Funciones de las Misiones Culturales y Determinan sus Formas de Trabajo en General*, p. 3.

crops will be a cultural advance of hundreds of years over the theory of setting up rain gods, having seed blessed, and holding festivals for good crops while the seed is planted in poorly plowed ground and never cultivated, weeded, or irrigated. Training is given the teacher in social investigation and organization. That is, he is trained to survey his local social group and find definite needs and then to organize the people to work for the realization of their social desires. These socially approved aims cover such things as reforestation, domestic and social hygiene, and the suppression of vice, such as gambling, immorality, and drinking.

A second purpose of the Mission is to lead the rural teacher toward a nicer understanding of Scientific Socialism. Just as every segment of the Scientific Socialist school attempts to bring the students nearer their *capacitación,* so the Cultural Mission means to lead the *maestro* toward his own *capacitación* in philosophy. If the teacher understands the philosophy clearly he will develop new ways of teaching in consonance with the system. This philosophical training will tend to eliminate "fads" and blind copying of methods. The Mission proposes to give the instructor a proletarian consciousness and a feeling of personal responsibility in the creation of a new order. A feeling of the great role the teacher plays in the scheme of rehabilitating a people is communicated to the teaching body. They are to be fired like the ancient crusaders with a zeal to build a new world; but, unlike the crusaders, they are to call upon reason and brotherhood instead of blind emotion, fanaticism, and bloodshed. As a part of his Socialist *capacitación* the teacher is changed from an individualistic thinker to a co-operative thinker. That is, he is taught the body of knowledge and shown the positions that have been accepted as the result of years of thought.

He is then shown how to subordinate his selfish thinking to the philosophy that is working for a slow common betterment. Lastly he is led to free his own thinking within the limits of Socialism so that he can make newer and richer contributions to the body of social thought. Above all, the teacher is freed from the hold of superstition, dead custom, and fanaticism so that he can help free the minds of his people.

Eventually standards will be established for all rural teachers, demanding that a minimum amount of education be required. At present and for the past sixteen years the schools, starting from practically nothing, have grown so rapidly that no such demands can be made. Add to the difficulty of getting teachers in the first place the fact that two thousand teachers yearly drop from the ranks,[5] and it becomes evident that anyone with the slightest smattering of formal learning must be pressed into service.[6] Another goal of the Cultural Missions, that of helping teachers work for a normal-school diploma, is reached by allowing them to take examinations in the required fields of learning. After a series of institutes many teachers are prepared for these examinations and the median of teacher standards is thus raised.

The Mission functions as a supervisory aid in its district. There are district inspectors and supervisors, and with these the Mission works intimately. An attempt is made to keep the number of teachers attending each institute down to sixty. Such limiting allows a record to

[5] Ignacio García Tellez, *La Función de las Misiones Culturales ante la Reforma Educativa*, p. 2.

[6] Ignacio García Tellez, *Socialización de la Cultura*, p. 53, estimates that 35,000 teachers are required today. Statistics are difficult to obtain; but *Revista de Educación*, Septiembre de 1937, gives 14,743 as the total of the rural school teachers. Teachers in other departments can hardly total 5,000. See also Nathaniel and Sylvia Weyl, *The Reconquest of Mexico* (Oxford University Press, New York), chapter xii.

be kept of the preparation of each teacher so that he can be given counsel in his teaching and shown the additional training he needs. As the members of the Mission make a specialized study of the region in which they work, they are in a position to know, over a period of time, whether the teaching in that region is accomplishing what it is intended to accomplish. Conferring with both supervisors and teachers, they are thus able to co-ordinate the work of the entire region, strengthening the position of the supervisors and encouraging the teachers.

The Mission adds weight to the position of the *maestro,* for the inertia of the peasantry might force him to abandon his plans for establishing the new order. School leaders expect the repeated impacts of the fresh body of "shock troopers" to overcome this social lag and to educate the people slowly into a new way of thinking and doing. Each time a Mission comes to a place, it leaves permanent records of its stay. Besides the material changes it makes in the form of water filters, better houses, and model fields, there are organizations set up that continue functioning after the Mission has left. There are branches of the Bank of Agricultural Credit for the benefit of the *ejidos* and co-operative farmers, and committees of health, sanitation, and infant care.

One important work of the Cultural Mission is to serve as an agency to spread the ideas of Socialism and to explain it and to gain friends for the government's program. Thus they hope to counter the propaganda spread by the Church and the large haciendas and wealthy groups. The constitutional rights of the people are explained to them, particularly their agrarian rights and their rights as workers to organize and demand better working conditions, higher wages, and shorter hours. The program of the Secretary of Education is also explained to the people. They are shown the actual work of the schools, how they are attempting to ameliorate the living conditions of the proletariat and to make better beings of them economically, socially, and morally. There is still a vast body of vicious propaganda to overcome. Mexico, like other civilized countries, has her "whispering campaigns," rumors, gossips, and slanders, most of them emanating from established centers. The author has been told by many well-intentioned Mexicans in all seriousness that the Socialist teachers have been recruited from brothels, opium dens, and other centers of vice for the sole purpose of teaching sex and attacking the Church. The work of the Missions, made up of soft-spoken, clear-eyed men and women who go about their work with sympathy, tact, and understanding, goes a long way to disprove these stories.[7]

Cultural Missions serve somewhat the same purpose as did the troubadours and wandering minstrels of a past day. They go from village to village spreading a gospel of beauty. They bring music, literature, popular and plastic arts, games and regional sports, and dances. They attempt to keep alive the beauty that has always been a part of Mexico, while they separate from the wheat of beauty the chaff of bigotry, cruelty, immorality, and superstition. Worth-while folklore, legend, *corrido,* and stories are carried from one section to another. Many of these stories are old, beautiful legends having a historic and literary value that makes them worth saving. New stories and songs are introduced that have a different moral from the old Mexican tale that was always incrusted with the supernatural. New stories have a moral, showing the value of living clean, working together, and

[7] Frank Tannenbaum, *Peace by Revolution,* p. 296; Katherine M. Cook, *The House of the People,* p. 27.

adopting modern ways of doing things. A victrola, a radio, and moving-picture apparatus are part of the equipment of the Mission. Each evening the villagers are entertained with music and pictures. The cinema in Mexico has already reached a high degree of art and is popular with the people. Like the art and architecture of Mexico, it is functional, a part of the people. Highly paid artists are not included in the cast. Generally one or two professional actors are used in the making of a picture and the remainder come from the everyday people of a region. "Janitzio," such a moving picture of the life and customs of the Tarascan fishermen of the Lake Patzcuaro region, is rapidly becoming a classic in the world of the cinema.

Preparation of the cultural missioners.—Today the *misioneros* are prepared as thoroughly for their forays into the hinterland as is an army preparing for a campaign. During their training period they spend day after intensive day in the Secretaría de Educación Pública, acquiring new knowledge, steeping themselves more thoroughly in the philosophy and ideology of the school system, and learning techniques that have been developed on the far-flung battle front of the campaign against ignorance and poverty. The author sat with these *misioneros* through part of their training period. Experts in all lines lectured and demonstrated to them in the fields of folk art, hygiene, dietetics, and the psychology of working with backward peoples. The primary emphasis is always upon the economic betterment of the people.[8] Each group has as nearly a homogeneous section of country to work in as possible. This country is studied thoroughly, so that the greatest possible exploitation of its natural resources can be made under the direction of the Mission.

[8] Ignacio García Tellez, *La Función de las Misiones Culturales ante la Reforma Educativa,* p. 1.

Dentro de la orientación de la Escuela Socialista, la capacitación del maestro requiere estar estrechamente vinculada con la función económica de medio, no solo para adaptarse a él, sino principalment para transformarlo, mejorando las condiciones de la producción.[9]

This institution is designed, par excellence, for the teaching of co-operation and the development of local leadership. The missioners and local *maestros* and the community work together in such close interrelationship, they have such a community of interests, and so constantly exchange what they have learned, that co-operation becomes a living reality. The ideal of the highly socialized teacher is ever uppermost in the minds of the directors of the Cultural Mission. They have learned from the bitter experience of the Church that it is not sufficient to teach by precept. Each teacher, if the Institute of Socialist Orientation working through the Cultural Mission has its way, will be a walking exemplar of the new era.

The new teacher is a loyal friend, a good counsellor, a knight at the service of the work of social renovation. The teacher is, at the same time, a conductor, a guide of children and adolescents, and for this he requires as a basic condition: scientific capacity, absolute probity. A living exemplar, he must make of his life a moral example; it is not enough that the educator be a man of science, it is necessary that he live publicly and privately in accord with social morality—not with the conventional hypocritical bourgeois morality, but with a sturdy moral creed of human assistance.[10]

Mexico has been divided into districts, each of which is as nearly uniform geographically, economically, and ethnically as possible. One traveling Mission covers each territory, and the workers thus become expert in the needs and language of the territory. The missioners have been

9 *Ibid.*
10 Ignacio García Tellez, *op. cit.*, p. 3. Translation by the author.

forced to learn the Indian dialects in order to carry forward their work more efficiently.

One of the strictest charges laid upon the missioners before they leave for their field work is that of using the greatest tact and patience at all times. They must allay the suspicions of Indians accustomed to trickery and exploitation when dealing with any form of government. They are confronted with deliberate campaigns to vilify the schools; the Scientific Socialist school is presented in the mercenary press and in whispering campaigns as though it had no other object than to work, implacably, against religion. The worker is warned that he is not to be surprised or angered at any sudden, unjustified attack. He is not to answer in kind, and is to be courteous and thoughtful at all times. A constructive campaign must go forward to enlighten the people, remove their ignorance and superstition, and better their economic situation. While this campaign goes on, let the heathen rage:

Stay clear of the beaten track that leads through the field of declamation; to the attacks, to the calumnies, to the insidious remarks, we shall respond with the constructive work of the Socialist school, which shall become great through the enthusiastic co-operation of teachers and authorities motivated by a sane revolutionary spirit.[11]

The Cultural Mission in operation.—A Cultural Mission unit ordinarily consists of seven members: the *jefe* (or chief), a rural organizer, a woman social worker, a nurse, a music teacher, a teacher of plastic arts, and a moving-picture operator. The *jefe* does not devote his time to administration alone; he is leader, teacher, co-ordinator, and social worker. Before leaving on a tour of duty he must confer with the Director of Federal Education and the Chief of the Department of Socialist Orientation

[11] Ignacio García Tellez, *op. cit.* (author's translation), p. 7.

and outline his prospective work. He then has a conference with the Inspector of the zone in which he will work. After this groundwork is complete he oversees the actual preparation—the loading of the truck with the necessary equipment, the designating of the place to work and the route to be followed. After the group arrives at the village which will be its home for the following six or eight weeks, the *jefe* becomes a social worker and teacher. He teaches Socialist orientation, history of the proletarian movement in Mexico, the international workers' movement, the unequal distribution of Mexico's wealth, the religious problem in Mexico, and the educational policy of the Secretary of Public Education.

The rural organizer works with the community and with the teachers. His work with the community consists of promoting the renovation and construction of better homes; supervising the distribution and use of water for home use and irrigation; improving the livestock situation; stimulating the planting of trees; and establishing community services. These community services consist of pioneering the establishment of a medical center, post office, telephone line, better markets and a hygienic slaughterhouse, public lighting, and a public park. He is also active in organizing guilds in the community. The rural organizer gives courses to the teachers on the federal labor law, the Agrarian Code, and the texts of laws covering agricultural credit and allied subjects. While the Mission is in the community, he takes charge of school gardens and demonstrates methods to students, teachers, and citizens.

The nurse takes the lead in hygienic betterment and trains the local midwives in simple methods of cleanliness and sanitation. She teaches groups of adults the deleterious effects of alcohol and the causes, prevention, and cure of venereal diseases, and gives them the theory and a practical demonstration of vaccination. She increases the teachers' knowledge of health and medicine. The woman social worker functions in close co-operation with the nurse and the rural organizer.

The moving-picture operator is on call at all times with his machine, showing pictures that demonstrate the manifold activities of the *misioneros*. The teacher of music and the teacher of plastic arts not only bring music and art to the people; they organize that of the people. The physical-education teacher handles games, sports, dances, and festivals among adults, children, and teachers. He organizes teams and competitions for intervillage rivalry. This healthy competition tends to break down centuries-old feuds between neighboring towns and adds to the feeling of co-operation and friendliness being engendered everywhere.

Originally the Missions operated only a month in one locality. As the number of Missions grew and as the work became better organized and more scientific, the period lengthened to six and even eight weeks. The first two weeks are devoted to studying the environment, getting acquainted with the folk and the teachers, and studying local politics and problems. The missioners adopt the local dress and become part of the country. After this preliminary skirmish the institute is established and operated for four or five weeks. At the close of the training period examinations are given in the academic courses and unfinished business is cleared up. Then a grand *fiesta* is held, a *fiesta* of a type new to Mexico. Here the people are encouraged to take part in activities that build health and good feeling. No longer does the peasant go about with a bottle in one hand and a knife in the other. Health, happiness, and friendship are the patron gods of this festival. It is a celebration of the work that is finished and of

The old and the new in Mexico. Ixtaccihuatl seen from the modern Mexico—Puebla Highway.

Physical education teachers in Mexico's new schools.

A group of hikers on a Sunday climb. The schools promote healthful activities such as this for children and adults.

the work that is just beginning. An official representative of the United States Office of Education gives a splendid description of one of these *fiestas*.

When the month's work of the cultural mission and its local group of teachers end, the closing day is a fiesta occasion for the immediate community in which the institute is held and for the surrounding region whose schools are represented in the attendance. The opportunity to participate in and observe the closing day of a teacher's institute conducted by the mission at Tula was a revelation to the author in the amount of and spirit of community interest, and especially in the fact that participation extended well beyond the immediate community, being truly representative of the region at large. Tula is an ancient city, once a center of pre-Hispanic civilization and obviously a city of dignity and importance during and since the Spanish régime. Arriving there on the morning of the closing day, one felt the festive and hospitable atmosphere. Buildings were decorated with flags; streets were filled with horses and cattle on their way to the exhibits, and with men, women, and children, riding and on foot; food was cooking and on sale along the streets and in the market square —a typical Mexican fiesta spirit everywhere in evidence.

A street fair surrounded the market square, exhibiting products of the neighboring *haciendas* and *ejidos,* horses, cattle, chickens, vegetables, and fruits attractively, even amazingly, arrayed, many of the animals carrying the prize ribbons recently won. Horses and cattle were decorated with ribbons and flowers, some in ancient Aztec patterns preserved and used continuously through the centuries and of traditional or religious significance to the descendants of the early civilizations.

The institute itself had prepared an extensive exhibit of its work, forecasting the activities which during the coming school year would be featured by the teachers in attendance at their respective schools. The institute exhibit was made up of products of the school gardens, canned fruits and vegetables, all types of handicrafts including furniture, baskets, pottery, weaving, and the like, industries which the next year the teachers would be promoting in their school communities.

In the morning there were games, athletic stunts, native dances in which teachers and community participated and which were given in the village stadium, again forecasting and demonstrating the activities which teachers would be expected to promote through their schools in the local communities to which they would later be assigned or from which they came. In the afternoon the guests were entertained by a performance at the theater, consisting chiefly of short 1-act plays, music, native dances, and the like.[12]

The Cultural Mission may be called the catalyst that is hurrying the combination of elements in Mexico, the flux that aids the welding of a people. It is an in-service teacher-training device, but it is much more than that. It is the apotheosis of Mexico's experimental institutions, it is an integration of economics, morals, science, and humanity. It is the thread on which are strung the varicolored beads of the peoples of Mexico, making of them a complete unity.

CENTROS DE EDUCACIÓN INDÍGENA[13]

For four centuries the Indian in Mexico has remained unconquered and unassimilated. True, he has been defeated and harried and dispossessed and enslaved; but he has never been conquered. Such a statement does not mean that the Mexican Indian is a fierce, untractable creature. On the contrary, he is usually a sensitive, artistic individual, finely attuned to nature. He has been bestialized, in many cases, by contact with a civilization that was morally and intellectually inferior to his own. "They denied to the Aztecs (their superiors mentally, morally, and in civilization) even the gift of reason."[14] Today the Indian

[12] Katherine M. Cook, *The House of the People*, p. 28.
[13] "Centers of Indigenous Education."
[14] Cora Walker, *Cuatemo, Last of the Aztec Emperors*, p. 342. Quoted from Judge Ignacio Ramirez.

remains to be reckoned with. He is not a noble savage, waiting to ambush travelers and scalp his enemies. He has retired as far into himself as possible. His resistance is passive; he is a brake on the vehicle of progress. Mexico's problem is to incorporate the Indian into the life of the country, and to make him an individual.

To succeed, therefore, Mexico must retain the spiritual structure of the Indian, and at the same time provide him with the necessities of a scientific technique which cannot be improvised. It must profit by the utilitarian forces of nature, and (taking them out from exploitation) improve the external conditions of life.[15]

House of the native student.—Through the efforts of Dr. Puig Casauranc a residence school was established in the suburbs of Mexico City for the education of Indian students. Here more than two hundred native youth were gathered from the twenty-eight states. They represented twenty-five different tribes and spoke as many languages. The first school was intended to demonstrate that the Indian could be educated and to train leaders who would return to their people and act as guides in leading them toward a higher plane of culture. In the first aim the school succeeded admirably; in the second it was a dismal failure. The students were taught Spanish and were trained in advanced handicrafts and petty industries. They learned modern games and gymnastics, and competed wholeheartedly. Academic learning came easily for them, and they soon adopted the Europeanized methods of living in the capital city. But when the time came for the student to return to his people, the plan broke down. The Indian had become too well incorporated into Mexican life. He wanted to continue living in or near the urban centers;

[15] William Gates, *Rural Education in Mexico and the Indian Problem,* p. 22.

he wanted to be an automobile mechanic or a storekeeper. The student had helped construct his own hygienic quarters with running water and sanitary living surroundings. He had no desire to return to the *jacales* of his people and live with the animals on a dirt floor with the rain dripping through on his grimy body.

This first Casa del Estudiante Indígena was far from being a loss to Mexican education, however. It was followed by other schools in different parts of the nation and through this progression came the knowledge necessary to plan the new type of work. As other schools were founded it became evident that as the school neared the country of the autochthons the results obtained became more pronounced. A larger and larger percentage returned to their own people to add a nucleus of civilization to the primitives. Other factors now entered the problem. Students brought back knowledge that was useless in this new environment. Too, it became evident that a few isolated individuals could not greatly affect the inertia of a backward people. The next link in the chain of logic was the establishment of centers in the midst of the Indian countries.

Establishment of the Indian centers.—The lesson learned from the House of the Indian Student was that he could be educated, but that he was being turned out as an individualist rather than as a co-operating member of a collectivist society. Professor Rafael Ramirez said of this experiment:

. . . . So we set about looking for more satisfactory methods that would integrate the Indians by groups and masses and not by individuals and, above all, that when they became integrated with civilized groups they should not become alienated from their intrinsic ideals and worthy types of life. . . . . The educational experiment brought about through the House of the Indigenous Student was not a failure. Everybody in

Mexico is now convinced that it is possible to educate the Indian because it is recognized that he has great capacity, and not only are we convinced of this truth, but also of the urgent necessity to do so.[16]

In 1933 the transition was made to the Centros de Educación Indígena. There were ten such centers established that year, each in the midst of the Indian group it intended to redeem. By the end of 1934 twelve new centers had been added to help incorporate such diverse peoples as the Tarahumaras, the Mixtecas, the Otomíes, the Totonacas, the Chamulas, the Mazaguas, the Huastecas, and the Mayas. During 1935 ten more centers grew up. In 1937 President Lázaro Cárdenas called a conference of all Directors of the *Internados,* and thirty-three responded.[17]

At the beginning of 1937 the Secretaría de Educación Pública established the *Departamento de Educación Indígena* with Carlos Basauri as *jefe.* The new chief is an authority on the life and culture of the autochthonous races of Mexico. He is the author of *Monografía de los Tarahumares; Tojolabales, Tzeltales y Mayas,* and *La Situación Social de la Población Indígena; Estudio Etnográfico de los Tarascos;* and *Estudio Económico-Etnográfico de los Otomíes.*

Plan of action of the Indian centers.—Señor Basauri plans all his programs on the premise that there are two fundamental types of Indian culture: the static, that was checked by the Spaniards and that has remained in a more or less dormant stage; and the decadent, that, in its biologic, social economic, or political factors, had started breaking down before the conquest.[18]

---

[16] Quoted by George I. Sanchez, *op. cit.,* pp. 154–55.

[17] "Los Centros de Educación Indígena," *El Maestro Rural,* Julio de 1937.   [18] Carlos Basauri, *Centros de Educación Indígena.*

The Indian center is established in some spot that shows possibilities for future development from an agricultural or economic point of view. Soil, transportation, hygienic conditions, and nearness of raw materials are considered in choosing a site. This preliminary study is carried on by experts furnished by the Secretariat rather than by the faculty of the center.

In constructing the plant the underlying philosophy of Mexican education is followed. The buildings must be in keeping with the psychology of the region and the people. Materials easy to obtain are used and edifices that are sanitary and commodious are built. As the Indians are frequently semi-nomad, they do not work well if they feel too confined; so none of the buildings partake of the nature of a convent or barracks. Frequently the rooms have three sides, one side being open to the air and sunshine. The entire *centro* is built in the form and style of a well-designed proletarian village. Instead of large-capacity dormitories, the students are quartered in small houses accommodating six to eight. Larger structures are erected for shops, tool sheds, barns, or machine shops. There is one central building with classrooms and a general auditorium. An open-air theater is provided where singing, dancing, and theatricals may be held.

The Indian center is not a school in the traditional or classical understanding of the term. It might better be called a cultural colony, for the purpose is almost entirely one of social and cultural propaganda and training. It does not compete with the *escuela rural* which is being established in increasing numbers in Indian communities. The *internado* takes students of an older age and attempts to move them forward at an accelerated pace of development. The aim of the *internado* is to "streamline" evolution. Boys between the ages of fourteen and twenty, and girls between the ages of twelve and eighteen are enrolled in the center. The faculty consists of a director, a woman nurse, an agent of Indian organization, one teacher of general materials, one woman economist, and four teachers of arts, crafts, and petty industries. The first step in the education of the Indian youth is to teach them Spanish. Afterward the students are taught to build their own house—not as an academic exercise, but for the purpose of having a home. The students merely live and go their daily round of working, singing, dancing, playing games, and getting on with comrades. The only difference between the life in the *internado* and in an advanced community is the fact that the students are guided rapidly and naturally into more advanced techniques. There is just enough instruction and group work to remove the learning from the field of trial and error. In reality the center is almost purely a school of work. Students are not the graduates of the rural schools but are ones who have been missed by the schools.

The Department of Indigenous Education makes the point constantly that the centers are not an end in themselves, not a permanent form of education; they are rather a means to bridge the gap between pre-Conquest cultures and twentieth-century problems. The aim is the same as that in every other department of the present Mexican government—to keep the best of the Indian characteristics and habits and to add the most modern techniques of production. Machinery is brought to the centers and its use taught the Indians; but the thought is always uppermost in the minds of the teachers and is often expressed by them that the machine is for the use of man. The Indians are taught the usual lessons of modern socialization: the land is theirs, they must take it, keep it, and work it in the most efficient manner possible. They must not make production a god and themselves slaves to efficiency; on the other hand, they must release themselves from the slavery to the *maiz*. They must not work from daylight until dark with primitive tools to raise a small crop of low-grade corn so that their wives can spend all the day and half the night grinding the corn meal in a primitive mill. They are taught to raise diversified crops by using horses or mules and a steel plow and other modern tools. They are then taught how to get farm animals and tools by forming agricultural credit co-operatives and borrowing the money from the government. They are taught to form co-operatives that unite with national groups for the marketing of the crops advantageously. These techniques are not taught in lectures or speeches; the young men and women actually do all these things under the direction of their teachers. And the organizations they form are not junior groups or school groups; they are actually functioning co-operatives.

The students usually stay two or three years in the *centro*. When one leaves he may do one of two things: He can return to his own family, which may be some distance away, and put into practice the lessons learned. Or he may settle down as a part of the Indian center and with the help of his friends in the group and with the active guidance of the faculty build a house there for himself. Here he may marry and become a part of the community that knows how to work together, play together, and in general live together in an intelligent fashion. When the time comes that the community is a large, well-knit group, living the principles of Scientific Socialism, the faculty of the *internado* will quietly move out, so as to disturb no part of the social machinery, and start a new center in a location that has not yet felt the impact of the new education.

Temple of Quetzalcoatl

Typical market scene, Tlaxcala

Monument to an industrial hero, Hermosillo, Sonoro. (Photo by B. Wildman)

Chapter VII

SUMMARY

EVERYWHERE in Mexico, "*educar es redimir.*" Chiseled in the stone of monuments and school buildings; painted on murals, placards, and banners; and written in every book having to do with Mexico's schools, this motto epitomizes the philosophy of Socialist education. The present government of Mexico will stand or fall on the platform: "To educate is to redeem."

A new Mexico is on the march today. A Mexico that is searching the world for new truths and that attempts to evaluate everything in the light of science—not a science to set up as a golden calf for the people to worship but a science that shall be a genius waiting to serve the people. For the Mexican theory is that the people in Mexico are sovereign. No longer does official Mexico look upon the *gente* as hewers of wood and drawers of water for the few. The nation is striving for freedom for the individual and for herself, freedom from foreign domination in the field of ideas and in the field of economic exploitation. And education is the magic lamp which Mexico hopes will produce a genius to furnish this freedom.

When one attempts to judge the actual functioning of the Socialist schools of Mexico, he is immediately faced with contradictory impressions. A picture of the scores of modern school plants scattered over Mexico, filled with healthy, intelligent children, imbues the observer with enthusiasm. Other pictures of half-wild little savages in abandoned convents and adobe buildings leave one a little *triste*. One is reminded of Dr. Johnson's remark about the dog which walked on its hind legs: the remarkable thing is not how well the dog walks but that he walks so at all.

Human beings are pretty well alike the world over. The members of the teaching staff of Mexico's schools, the inspectors, and the directors are not a homogeneous body of Socialists, agreed in their methodology. The system is supposed to be flexible enough so that it can be changed as conditions change and new leaders with more advanced training come along. Many teachers are trying to change the system to fit their own whims at all times. Within the official family are many teachers not in accord with the objectives as laid down by the Secretariat. The leaders in Mexico City appear to be almost uniformly of a high type, morally, intellectually, and socially, and are bursting with enthusiasm; but as one visits schools on all levels he continually finds the pedestrian, routinized teacher conducting class in a manner typical of education of a past era. Many things that Mexico is doing and feels she has discovered have been done well and quite generally in the United States.

The author has regularly been told the same thing by experts in various lines of pedagogy who have visited schools with him or told of other experiences. In one school an American teacher will be overcome by amazement and admiration at some phase of work and remark, "They're years ahead of us." Yet next door may be an exhibition of "muddling through" that could easily be corrected by a knowledge of what has been worked out elsewhere. Mexico's attitude concerning education in the United States is an interesting compound of half-information and half-legend. It is generally believed that the schools of her northern neighbor are all housed in sumptuous buildings but that their education is of a highly reactionary nature. It would seem that Mexico can definitely profit by a thorough study of what has been done and is being done in the United States. Many of the leading educators have been trained in American universities and have taken back much with them. The fact remains that the entire body of educators is not cognizant of the fact that many progressive techniques are available next door.

Some of the rural schools might well serve as examples of a perfect blending of the useful and the beautiful. They are cheaply but well constructed, combining all the desirable features for school buildings embodied in the Socialist concept of education: maximum air and sunshine, functional design, and beauty of execution. Well-cared-for potted plants are everywhere, fruit trees abound, bees from the school aviary hum lazily in the blossoms. Carefully weeded and cultivated gardens stretch away on every side.

Other rural schools present a dreary appearance, perfectly described by the Mexican adjective, *triste,* "sad." A severely whitewashed adobe may sit in a wide expanse of plain with the foreground and background unbroken by tree or shrub. Windows are broken and unmended. A few anemic plants are stuck in the ground as though a sop to the national program of school gardens. Inside, old-style desks are arranged haphazardly on a dirty floor flanked by chipped walls and gray blackboards. However, it is only fair to say that this type of school is more typical of the northern states, which have long tried to build on lines similar to those of the United States. Here it is harder to change the school than it is to build one where there has never been a school before.

The important fact that one must keep in mind, however, is that Mexico is building schools. Poor schools can be improved and weak teachers can either be strengthened while in service or later replaced with stronger ones. Socialist education is not a theoretical plan that exists on paper only, nor is it an emasculate philosophy that is argued by cloistered savants. It is a program of action, formulated and reformulated by strong, athletic men and women who live the theory they advocate. *Maestros* who have lived and taught for months with a pistol always strapped on their hips are not inclined to be overly theoretical. Every point that is discussed at an institute or regional meeting represents a living experience to these people. Every month, almost every day, the program is being altered to meet actual practice. Every day more schools are being erected; every day more children are entering school who would never have had a chance to go to any school under the *ancien régime*.

And that is all that the observer can objectively report on the system. Mexico is providing the best schools that can be provided, and she is steadily trying to improve them. Only time can tell whether or not they will accomplish the redemption of a race that has seldom known anything but tyranny, oppression, and exploitation.

Appendix

MEXICAN VOCABULARY

Aguamiel—The unfermented juice of the maguey, from which pulque is made.

Aguardiente—Intoxicating liquor.

Ahuehuetl—Aztec drum.

Alcoholismo—Alcoholism.

Anáhuac—Ancient name of Mexico.

Amo—Master or overseer.

Antojitos—Typical prepared dishes of Mexico.

Arroyo—Ravine or river bed.

Audiencia—Vice-royal council and colonial supreme court maintained by Spain in her colonies.

Barranca—Gully or deep cut.

Besket-bol—Basketball.

Biblioteca Nacional—National library.

Buen vecino—Good neighbor.

Cacique—Native Indian chief; a political boss.

Caciquismo—Practice of native chiefs of exploiting their own people.

Calpisque—Native overseer on colonial *haciendas*.

Calpolli—Aztec community.

Campesino—Farmer.

Cantina—Saloon.

Capacitación—Capacity of any individual to be developed.

Carriles—Communal wood lots.

Casa de Azulejos—House of tiles; famous tourist center in Mexico City.

Casa del Estudiante—House of the native student; an experimental school.

Carcel de Belén—An infamous prison destroyed by the post-revolution government.

Casa del pueblo—House of the people; a name for the schools.

Cenotes—Natural wells in the limestone of Yucatan.

Centrales Agrícolas—Agricultural centers.

Centros de Educación Indígena—Centers of Indian education.

Conquistadores—Spanish conquerors.

Correctos—The genteel stratum of society.

Corridos—Songs of current happenings.

Cristero—"Followers of Christ." Guerrilla bands who killed government followers and burned schools.

Criollo—Pure Spaniard born in Mexico.

Cristo—Christ or image of Christ.

Diezmo—The tenth of a person's income or produce formerly taken by law for the church.

"Educar es redimir"—"To educate is to redeem."

Ejidos—Communal land plots.

Encomenderos—Proprietors of the great estates who owned the people on the land as well as the land.

Encomienda—A royal land grant with slaves.

Escuela de acción—School of action.

Escuela preparatoria—Preparatory school; an older type of school that is being superseded by the secondary school.

Escuelas mixtas—Coeducational schools.

Estado actuante—The activating state.

Ficha—Permanent record card kept for each student; file.

Fiesta—Festival with a religious basis featuring music.

Gachupine—Spaniard born in Spain.

Gente—People.

Gente de razón—Reasoning or rational people; genteel folk.

Global—Integral.

Hacendado—Rancher; owner of an hacienda.

Hacienda—Large estate.

Hectar—Approximately 2½ acres.

Huapango—Regional dance of Mexico's west coast.

Huéhuetl—Ancient trees of Cypress family.

Huelga—Strike.

Huitzilopochtli—Warlike god of Aztecs.

Igualación—Equalization.

Indio—Indian.

Jacal—Poor house; shack.

Jarabe—National dance of Mexico.

Jarana—Musical instrument and dance of Yucatan.

Jardín de niños—Kindergarten.

Jefe—Chief.

Jícaras—Lacquered wooden platters or trays from Michoacan.

Laca—Indigenous lacquer work.

La Trinchera—The Trench; a part of Orozoco's mural at the preparatory school.

Latifundias—Great land holding held out of use.

Ley fuga—Law of flight; permits captors to shoot prisoner allegedly trying to escape.

Los de abajo—Those of the lower classes; title of book by Manuel Azuelo.

Lucha de clases—Class struggle.

Maestra—Female teacher.

Maestro—Male teacher.

Maguey—Century plant, from which fibers and juice are obtained.

Maíz—Field corn.

Mariachi—Stringed musical instrument; also applied to orchestra made up of stringed instruments.

Mesa central—Central plateau of Mexico.

Mescal—Intoxicating drink.

Mestizo—Half-Spaniard, half-Indian.

Metate—Flat stone on which corn is ground.

México típico—Typical Mexico.

Milpa—Cornfield.

Misioneros—Missioners; early untrained teachers.

"Mucho trabajo, poco dinero; Tengo frijoles, viva Madero"— Jingle from time of Madero—"Plenty of work, not much money; beans to eat, hurrah for Madero."

Muy hombre—Very much the man.

Orfeones—Musical clubs.

Paisano—Native countryman.

Palacio de bellas artes—Palace of Beaux Arts.

Partido nacional revolucionario—P.N.R.—National Revolutionary party.

Pastales—Communal grazing land handed down from Aztec Empire.

Pelado—Poor person; literally, "skinned one."

Peón—One forced to work out a debt.

Pinole—Ground, toasted corn.

Plan sexenal—Six-year plan.

Población—Small town.

Político—Politician.

Porfirismo—System of Porfirio Díaz.

Posole—Gruel made from corn.

Potrero—Water-hole.

Pronunciamento—Revolutionary pronouncement.

Pueblo—Town.

Pulque—Fermented juice of the maguey plant.

Pulquería—Place where pulque is sold.

Pelota—Ball for games.

Quetzalcóatl—White god of the Aztecs who left Mexico with a promise to return; the Spaniards were thought to fulfill this prophecy.

Ranchería—Small ranch.

Ranchero—Rancher.

Rebozo—Head covering; a shawl.

Rio Bravo—Rio Grande River.

Rurales—National police of Díaz used for political purposes as well as for crime suppression.

Sandunga—Dance of Tehuantepec.

Santos—Saints or images of saints.

Ser plenario—Full man.

Sindicato de Maestros Socialistas—Syndicate of Socialist School Teachers.

Son—Music for dance.

Tenochtitlán—Aztec name for Mexico City.

Teocalli—Aztec temple.

Teponaztli—Form of Aztec drum.

Tepozton—God worshiped anciently near Tepoztlan.

Tezontle—Red volcanic rock found on the central plateau, used extensively for building.

Tierra—Land.

Tierra caliente—Hot country.

Tierra fría—Cold country.

Tierra templada—Temperate country.
Tierra y libertad—Land and liberty.
Tilma—Indian carrying net.
Tlachiquero—Man who sucks juice from maguey plant.
Tlalocs—Weather gods.
Tontos—Ignorant people; lower classes.
Triste—Sad; applied to places where conditions are poor, especially sleepy villages.
Veterano—Veteran of the Revolution.
Vihuela—Musical instrument, same as mariachi.
Vitalismo—Psychologic behaviorism.
Zapatear—To tap time to music with the foot.
Zapatistas—Followers of Zapata.

INDEX

DATE DUE